A FORUM ON FINANCE

A FORUM ON FINANCE

EDITED BY

GEORGE B. ROBERTS
FOR THE SCHOOL OF BUSINESS
OF COLUMBIA UNIVERSITY

NEW YORK : MORNINGSIDE HEIGHTS
COLUMBIA UNIVERSITY PRESS
1940

FOREIGN AGENTS: Oxford University Press, Humphrey Milford, Amen House, London, E. C. 4, England, and B. I. Building, Nicol Road, Bombay, India; Maruzen Company, Ltd., 6 Nihonbashi, Tori-Nichome, Tokyo, Japan

MANUFACTURED IN THE UNITED STATES OF AMERICA

Foreword

THIS VOLUME contains fifteen addresses delivered before the evening Banking Seminar of the School of Business of Columbia University during the academic year 1938–39. By way of foreword, a brief review of the history and activities of the seminar would seem to be appropriate.

The Banking Seminar has been a part of the life of Columbia University since 1920. Organized originally by the late Dr. H. Parker Willis, it remained under his guidance and inspiration until his death in July, 1937. From the beginning the seminar has met weekly, in the evening, the first meetings being held in Kent Hall at the university, before the School of Business building was constructed. In the conduct of meetings, Dr. Willis at the outset adopted a policy, to which he adhered consistently, of sharing the leadership of the discussion with outside speakers and with members of the seminar who were prepared to present the results of their research.

In the fall of 1932 Dr. Willis organized a day section, consisting of a small group of students who collaborated in the preparation of the volume entitled *The Banking Situation,* subsequently published under the joint authorship of Dr. Willis and Professor John M. Chapman. In the following year this group assisted in the preparation of Dr. Willis' book on *The Economics of Inflation,* and afterwards continued to meet as a group interested primarily in research. Thus in the course of time the day section became the banking research group, and in the fall of 1938 was formally recognized in the university catalogue as the Day Seminar, its work centering around the papers of students working for the degrees of Master of Arts, Master of Science, and Doctor of Philosophy.

Meantime the Evening Seminar has continued as an active forum for the discussion of problems and developments relating to banking, money, and credit. Following the death of Dr. Willis, the Evening Seminar was conducted jointly by Professors B. H. Beckhart, John M. Chapman, and Ralph West Robey, of the School of Business, until the fall of 1938, when the present writer assumed charge. With the concentration of research work in the Day Seminar in recent years, the program of the evening meetings has been given over to addresses by visiting speakers, followed in each case by a period of questions and general discussion. In this way there has been brought to the group a variety of thought and experience by experts and leaders, representative not only of the academic field but also of active business and banking and of government.

The present volume represents the first presentation of the seminar addresses in book form, where they will be available to other students as a permanent record. It is regretted that this collection is incomplete, in that six of the lectures delivered during the year are omitted, either in deference to the desire of the lecturer not to be quoted or because the speaker did not write out his address. Acknowledgment is due to those speakers, who, though unrepresented in this volume, nevertheless contributed in an important way to the work of the seminar. These speakers, together with the subjects of their addresses, were as follows: Roger Steffan, Vice President, The National City Bank of New York, "Modern Personal Credit"; Adrian M. Massie, Vice President, The New York Trust Company, "Investing for a Commercial Bank"; Dr. Otto Rosenberg, former Secretary, Austrian Bankers Association, "Vienna as a Financial Center"; Dr. F. Cyril James, Principal and Vice Chancellor, McGill University (formerly Professor of Finance, University of Pennsylvania), "Aspects of the Chicago Money Market"; Dr. Otto Nathan, Associate Professor of Economics, New York University, "Business Cycle Theory and Public Spending"; and William McC. Martin, Jr., President, The New York Stock Exchange, "The New York Stock Exchange."

To these men and to those whose addresses follow (in the order in which they were presented), the seminar owes a large debt of gratitude. It is the willingness of men of such caliber to give generously of their time and energy to educational work of this kind that has made possible the continuance of the seminar.

George B. Roberts

New York
February, 1940

Contents

A FORUM ON FINANCE

Shepard Morgan

Deficit Financing in Germany

I FEEL a good deal of diffidence about the subject I am supposed to discuss—an economic subject, and yet I am not an economist. Nevertheless I am about to try to elucidate some of the most occult mysteries of economics. So bear with me if I lose my way.

The topic I have in mind is briefly this: Why is it that the existing regime in Germany, starting with neither capital nor credit, has nevertheless carried through for a period of five years and more a colossal program of rearmament and material reconstruction, and yet has avoided almost entirely the normal penalties of inflation? According to accepted standards, the whole performance is an obscure and tantalizing mystery. We may object that the mystery of little or no inflation in Germany is no deeper than the mystery of little or no inflation thus far in the United States, where, as we all know, the economic material for an immense expansion of production and prices has been lying around for years, without realizing either the hopes of those who wanted inflation or the alarms of those who feared it.

The two situations are, of course, entirely different, and an attempt to analyse them both would not be productive, for to my mind neither has much bearing on the other. The reasons why the usual signs of inflation have been largely absent in both countries are peculiar to each and do not embrace corresponding causes. The situations differ principally in this respect, that while here executive action has been often directed toward producing a little inflation—"controlled inflation," as it is called—in Germany the full power of the executive has been aimed at preventing altogether the usual signs of inflation.

Probably no single act of government in Germany would produce today more violent opposition on the part of the people as a whole than precipitating inflation. This is due, of course, to the vivid memories the bulk of Germans now living still hold of the great inflation which ended in 1924. Even the Great War itself did not bear so heavily on the public at large as did the inflation, which closed, as we remember, with the currency revalued at the rate of a million million to one. The German inflation had three principal signs, each readily visible to the people. These were:

1. A rapidly rising price level;
2. A rapidly falling value of the mark in the foreign exchanges;
3. A rapidly rising bank-note circulation, coupled with an increasing shortage of hand-to-hand currency.

There were other manifestations of inflation, too, but they were mostly causal or collateral to the signs I have mentioned. And it is these signs that every German government since 1924, including the Hitler regime of the present, has been trying to avoid, for each has known that a recurrence of them would lead more or less promptly to its being thrown out. I myself believe that no German government, even one so powerfully intrenched as the National Socialist government of today, could long endure if inflation like the one still remembered should recur.

I do not need to explain that these are not the only earmarks of inflation. But they are the earmarks that are instantly perceived by the people as a whole. And it is for that reason that the full power of the National Socialist state has thus far been used, and used successfully, to prevent their showing themselves.

Other earmarks of inflation Germany unquestionably has, but they come, I think, rather under the head of expansion than inflation. Anyone who has ever attempted to make a definition of inflation which is at once exact and all-embracing, will see why I avoid the issue at this point, and classify these other earmarks as signs of expansion rather than inflation. I state them as follows:

1. A vast building and industrial activity, which looks to the visitor from abroad like the Coolidge prosperity of 1928. I was in Berlin as recently as July, 1938, and the scene impressed me then much as New York did in the summer of 1928, when I returned to this country briefly from Berlin—enormous building enterprises under way, whole sections of the city taken over by the wrecker to make room for new construction, immense activity on every side. Costs were expressed in terms of milliards of marks, rather than in terms of millions. Rebuilding operations on almost as grand a scale were in progress also in Munich and Hamburg. Furthermore, a whole new city was projected for the manufacture under public control and with public funds of a popular-priced automobile. They have taken as the site of the new city some thousands of acres of the best wheat land in Germany. In Berlin the public authorities have already taken title to plots of land in one of the best modern residential districts of the city, to serve as the new site for the Friedrich Wilhelm University. They tell you that it will have a frontage of about a mile and a half, and be the largest university in the world. These are merely examples of the soaring ambitions of the National Socialists, unrestrained, it would appear, by any considerations of cost.

2. Labor shortage. The very large and costly unemployment of former years has been converted into a shortage of both skilled and unskilled labor, even though working hours have been lengthened and many women have been taken back into employment. In order to deal with this shortage, and also, I assume, to prepare for the time when some hundreds of thousands of additional workmen would be needed for the new fortifications along the Rhine, a decree was issued in July, 1938, providing for the conscription and arbitrary allocation of labor, as the state might require. The

terms of the decree were so broad that they applied not to manual labor alone but to professional and executive workers also, if the government needed them for any purpose.

3. Material shortage. It is obvious that these gigantic operations of the state, which, as we have observed, include much outside the work of rearmament, put a terrific strain on the supply of materials. This strain was already acute by reason of the demands of rearmament and of Herr Goering's Four-Year Plan. The latter had as its primary objective making Germany self-sustaining and measurably independent of foreign raw materials, but the plants which had to be built were themselves enormously elaborate and required for their construction and equipment immense supplies of domestic as well as foreign materials. In consequence, rationing has long been in effect, not only of raw materials and finished products of domestic origin and fabrication, but of all products obtainable abroad. The result is a planned economy in the most stringent form. Practically no new projects can be undertaken by private individuals, firms, or corporations without explicit approval by the appropriate public authority. This applies not only to projects requiring foreign materials or goods, but to domestic undertakings as well. In all departments of industrial or business life, public enterprises have the right of way, and in order that there shall be no doubt about it, private enterprises are subjected to scrutiny, restraint, and delay, and often to prohibition.

This brief picture of the Germany in the face of 1938 gives some idea of the magnitude of the work in process, a grandiose program of construction, rehabilitation, and national development. Granted that the three factors I have mentioned—excessive industrial activity, acute labor shortage leading to conscription, and acute material shortage leading to rationing—are earmarks of the expansion aspect of inflation, why are the other earmarks of inflation still absent? Why is it that prices have remained relatively stable, that the value of the free mark in terms of dollars is precisely what it was in 1930, except for the appreciation due to our own devaluation, that the volume of hand-to-hand currency has not risen unduly? These are the points upon which the German public is most sensitive, because they remember bitterly the inflation of the early twenties, and it is precisely because of those bitter memories that the National Socialist state has gone to great lengths to prevent their recurrence. What, in fact, has it done?

The answer to that question is the substantial part of this discussion, and I shall now attempt to give it. Or rather, I shall divide the question into its three elements, and give the answer, as I see it, to each of the three.

First: Why has the German price level remained stable?

In April, 1933, shortly after the National Socialists came into power, the index of wholesale prices stood at 98.4, taking the 1913 level as 100. Five years later, that is to say in April, 1938, the index was 105.6. The rise was therefore roughly 7 percent, a sufficient testimony to stability. The country-wide level of retail prices is of course more difficult to determine, but my own impression, formed during many trips to Germany and against the background of a long residence there, is that retail prices have changed correspondingly little.

The measures used to accomplish this result were measures which only an authoritarian state could employ. In a democracy such as ours it would be entirely possible to pass a law prescribing the stability of prices, but to be effective Congress would have to pass not a law but a miracle. The National Socialist government of Germany not only made a law, but established controls to enforce it which Congress could not have authorized without violating the very soul of our liberties.

Control over prices in Germany is exercised by the Reich price commissioner. The final decision on all prices rests with him. It is his primary duty to keep prices in general as low as possible and to eradicate profiteering. On the other hand, he has permitted prices to rise whenever changing circumstances made it appropriate, thereby preventing economic development from being retarded. When allowing price rises in one department of the economy, he has, however, tried to equalize them as far as possible by effecting price reductions in other departments. By March, 1937, when world prices were around their peak, his task had become increasingly difficult, but since then the general fall in the prices of raw material has made it easier to maintain reasonably stable prices in Germany. And just as he succeeded in preventing economic development from being retarded by excessive price rises, he has succeeded in keeping prices within control at a reasonable level. It has been estimated by a competent American observer that if price controls were not in effect, prices would be between 30 and 40 percent higher than they are.

We might be interested in observing how price controls work in the case of a common household commodity, such as butter. A summer or two ago I was in Berlin and noticed outside the stores dealing in dairy products long lines of customers waiting for the chance to buy their allotments for the day. However good a customer and however willing one might be to pay a premium, both the allotment and the price were kept down to the prescribed amount. If the shopkeeper should accept a premium, both he and the customer would be liable to severe penalties. So one took what one could get or went without. It happened that a few days later I was walking in the Bavarian mountains and stopped in at a farmhouse to get lunch. To my surprise the lunch consisted mainly of bread, served with a loaf of butter almost the size of the bread itself. Thus was illustrated one of the reverse effects of price control. Had prices been permitted to take their natural course, that butter would have been attracted to Berlin, in response to demand implemented by price. But since no such attraction was felt, it remained in the mountains.

Wage scales, like prices, have remained under constant and

strict supervision. Since strikes are outlawed in Germany, higher wage scales cannot be obtained by this means. Wage rates in general have risen by only a negligible fraction, though the wage scales of a few categories of skilled workmen have latterly been allowed to increase beyond the average rise in wages, owing to the growing shortage of skilled labor. The sum total of wages, of course, because of the great increase in the number of employed persons, has risen very greatly—from around RM2,000,000,000 a month at the beginning of 1933 to nearly RM4,000,000,000 at present.

Second: Why has the foreign exchange value of the reichsmark remained relatively stable?

Again the answer is control, as exercised by an authoritarian state. But in giving that answer I hasten to say that the term stability applies only to one kind of mark, the so-called "free mark." This is the reichsmark which is ordinarily quoted in the newspaper at around 40 cents. It is the only mark upon the use of which, in Germany, there are no restrictions. The rate corresponds closely to the statutory gold content of the mark, in relation to the statutory gold content of the American dollar. It is precisely the same mark as the one established under the Dawes Plan, which for years maintained its value at around 23.8 cents. The higher price now quoted reflects no change in Germany, but the change which we ourselves brought about through the devaluation of the dollar.

But the free mark is only one of a dozen or so different kinds of marks. In recent years there have been as many as twenty-five or thirty different sorts of marks, but the number of varieties has latterly been reduced by consolidating some of the classifications. These non-free marks differ from one another according to the transactions from which they arise and according to the purposes to which they may be put. Their price in New York varies from about 3 cents for the so-called emigrant mark (which allows for the heavy taxation placed by Germany on the funds an emigrant takes with him) to about 19 cents for the registered mark and the travel mark, the use of which, in Germany, is restricted and subject to narrow regulation.

Now, it is obvious to anyone who thinks in terms of economics, that it is necessary to the preservation of the German economy to restrict the uses to which the various kinds of marks can be put. At the onset of the depression, as everyone knows, there was a vast accumulation of claims upon Germany in the shape of bank deposits, bonds of the Reich, German states, cities, and corporations, shares of stock in German industries, mortgage loans to Germany, and so on. Efforts were made in 1931, as we all know, for everyone to liquidate at once. The Reichsbank's supply of gold and foreign exchange was quickly depleted, and the transfer problem, which had lain dormant all during the life of the Dawes Plan, quickly roused itself and had to be dealt with. In part this was done by the foreign creditors themselves, who agreed with the German authorities to limit the amount and speed of their withdrawals, usually at material cost to themselves. In part it was done by the German government, which set up elaborate administrative controls over the foreign exchanges.

The enforcement of the government restrictions over foreign exchange transactions is centered in the Reichsbank and the Ministry of Economics. The double control has the effect of conserving the available supply of foreign exchange, but it delays transactions, both for the German who wants foreign money and for the foreigner who wants to move funds out of Germany. The demand, of course, is enormous and greatly exceeds the supply. The function of the control authorities is to apportion whatever foreign exchange comes into the country, as the result of export trade or otherwise, to those applicants who can prove the most valid need. This is a difficult and perplexing task, and anyone who has witnessed the efforts of these officials to arrive at a practicable conclusion in a disputed case does not envy them their work.

The foreign creditor is not their only adversary. Though his claims, collectively speaking, have been much reduced in the past seven years or so, the foreign creditor's total demands, both at long and short term, are still unmanageable if the current requirements of the German people, the German industries, and the German government are to be measurably met. No doubt the time will come when these foreign debts will be so far reduced that it will pay the German government to clear off the remnant and thereby restore shattered German credit. But that time is not yet in sight. At present, and perhaps for years to come, the foreign creditor—and I speak particularly of the creditor at long term—comes well down on the list of applicants for the available foreign exchange.

At the head of that list undoubtedly comes the government itself. During the rearmament process, the government needed and obtained, either directly or by furthering the demands of industries holding government contracts, foreign exchange for the purchase of such raw materials as iron ore, minerals for hardening steel, leather for shoes and saddles, copper, tin, and other metals, cotton and hemp, such finished products as aeroplane motors, tinned meats, rubber products, and so on. In addition to rearmament requirements, the government itself and the government-owned corporations continue to need, for the prosecution of the Four-Year Plan and the vast works of public construction, immense supplies of material from abroad, which put a further burden on the foreign exchanges.

Alongside the special needs of the government are of course the subsistence requirements of the people. German agriculture, except in the very best crop years, produces less in most categories of food than the population consumes. Thus, even allowing for the use of inferior grains and potatoes for flour, Germany ordinarily is a large importer of wheat. Similarly, Germany is deficient in live-stock production for food. And of course it has to import all its coffee and tea, all its southern fruits (to the extent that their importation is permitted at all), most of the lighter vegetables, and so on. In order to obtain such products, and in other departments wherever possible also, Germany resorts to many devices to conserve the stock of foreign exchange, including barter in more or less thinly disguised forms.

Third come the private requirements of industry. Even though German industry is the principal medium through which the national stocks of foreign exchange are replenished, no industry is permitted to use the proceeds of its exported products for its own purposes. As one leading manufacturer remarked, "We can't dispose of our own foreign exchange. It is all socialized. We have to pay it in to the Reichsbank, and if in our business we need a little of it we have to get permission like anybody else." The test applied to industrial applications for foreign exchange is mainly this: whether granting them will serve a national purpose; whether, for example, the foreign exchange sought for is necessary to carry out a government contract, or whether, upon being fabricated, raw materials purchased abroad will produce more foreign exchange than they cost. The use of foreign exchange to buy materials or goods abroad, which will go into the manufacture of goods designed for the private home market, is closely restricted.

Finally, the use of foreign exchange by travelers or departing emigrants is strictly controlled and the amounts allowed are so small as to fall far short of what we conceive to be normal travel requirements. As we all know, who have had occasion in recent years to pass the German frontiers, the so-called *devisen* control is more strict even than our own customs. German paper currency cannot legally be taken across the frontier, either by German citizens or foreigners, and the smallest penalty for infraction is confiscation and may be far more serious. Important instances of breaking the *devisen* regulations have been punished by long imprisonment or even death.

It is obvious from the foregoing that the National Socialist regime has employed all the resources of an authoritarian government to maintain the stability of the free mark. Furthermore, it is clear that if its regulations and enforcement were considerably relaxed, the values of the free mark and all the other marks would tend to merge at one figure, far below the nominal gold parity thus far maintained. Not only would that result alarm the people, but it would, in fact, precipitate those features of inflation which they most fear. It would deplete the country of existing stocks of goods, set in motion an accelerating rise of prices, reduce the purchasing power of the mark abroad, and release once again the devastating floods of inflationary currency.

That brings me to the third question: Why is it that the volume of hand-to-hand currency has not risen unduly?

Again the general answer is the authoritarian state, coupled with the skillful administration of the Reichsbank, carried through, I imagine, often against powerful opposition from within the National Socialist party. The specific answer is technical, but I shall attempt to make it as brief as possible.

In 1933, when the National Socialists came into power, their task was to reëstablish confidence, to find means for setting the economic machine in motion, and to provide the chances for work which they had promised their followers. The capital market was stagnant, and the only solution lay in utilizing the Reich's credit at short term. The prerequisite for this was not unfavorable, for the internal debt of the Reich was small.

A special cabinet committee met in May, 1933, under the chairmanship of Dr. Schacht, president of the Reichsbank, to outline what measures should be taken with regard to the money and capital markets. Among the things discussed was a contemplated decree for fostering reëmployment and financing it. Since little replacement had been effected by industry and agriculture in the three years preceding 1933, the decree offered far-reaching tax exemptions on replacements and improvements. But, above all, the government had mapped out for itself certain urgent tasks like road-building, agricultural betterment, the subsidizing of housing construction, and (even then) rearmament.

The decree for financing these tasks was published on June 1, 1933. Financing was to be done mostly through issuing "work-providing bills." Some of the bills later became known as "rearmament bills," since their proceeds were to be used exclusively for "reconstructing the defensive forces of the Reich." In general, however, both the "work-providing" and the "rearmament" bills are now referred to as "special bills" (*Sonderwechsel*).

The procedure was as follows: Whoever wished funds for public-works purposes made application to the Reich labor minister. If the application was approved, a certificate of authorization was issued. In its capacity as administrator of the work (the Reich, a state, a municipality, the German Railway Company, and so forth), the applicant drew a bill for the amount authorized on the Öffa (Deutsche Gesellschaft für öffentliche Arbeiten, which is owned by the Reich) or some other designated financing institution. After having had the Öffa or some other financing institution accept the "work bill," the administrator of the work gave it to the firm delivering the materials, and that firm appeared on the "work bill" as recipient. The recipient could pay his creditors with the work bill, or hold it, or have it discounted by one of the government-owned banks or by some other bank having relations with the Reichsbank. The Reichsbank was authorized to rediscount work bills. Holders received a return of anywhere between 3½ and 4 percent on them. These bills had a currency not exceeding three months. At maturity, they were presented to the drawee or acceptor, who was qualified to replace them with new work bills, again running for three months. The replacement or prolongation was effected as often as necessary until the bills were paid.

The government expected to redeem its bills in two ways: from rising revenues and from capital-market flotations. It had rightly calculated that the bills would give business a pronounced impetus and that tax receipts would mount accordingly. And it felt that the capital market would once more become productive, after the early uneasiness following the National Socialist seizure of power had abated.

The original decree stipulated that the issuance of these bills was to be limited to RM1,000,000,000. But as time went on and the rearmament program was expanded and accelerated, the issued amount of these bills exceeded RM1,000,000,000. Today several billion RM of such bills are outstanding, but the exact amount continues to be the secret of the German government. Many guesses have been made, both as to the total issue and the amount outstanding. A fair guess now might be around RM12,000,000,000 for the total, and say RM8,000,000,000 still outstanding. The issue of "special bills" was reported to have ceased as of March 31, 1938, after this method of interim financing had been in effect for rather less than five years.

Though tax revenues have been increasingly productive—I shall speak of taxes again a little later—it was obvious that the undertakings of the government must still rely on some substitute form of short-dated credit. Dr. Schacht foreshadowed the institution of a new form of bill at the annual meeting of the Reichsbank on March 11, 1938, when he said (I think somewhat euphemistically):

> The consolidation of economic conditions now makes it possible to abstain—in the field of supplying credit for Reich tasks—from the method of interim financing through special bills [Sonderwechsel] and to raise the necessary funds, in so far as they do not flow from the regular budget, through the direct placement of Reich Treasury certificates and Reich loans on the credit markets. In so far as Treasury bills are given in payment, this will be done only to the extent to which they can be

consolidated with ease when they mature. With the execution of this measure we have the guarantee that Germany's currency and finances will remain sound.

The treasury bills referred to by Schacht are *Lieferungsschatzanweisungen,* or treasury certificates of the Reich, given in payment for deliveries made to or on behalf of the Reich. They are also known by the short name "delivery certificates."

The issuing of these delivery certificates began soon after April 1, 1938. They are given in payment to contractors and firms making deliveries of goods and services to the Reich or its appointed agents, and have a currency of "approximately 6 months." While they are not eligible for rediscount at the Reichsbank, they may serve as collateral for loans from the Reichsbank (loans up to 75 percent of the value of the collateral; interest rate 5 percent). They are issued from time to time by the Reich Finance Minister, "in such amounts that their redemption will be assured on maturity."

Unlike the special bills, concerning which absolute secrecy is observed, the amount of delivery certificates outstanding is reported each month in the official monthly statement of the Reich finance ministry on the public debt of the Reich. They form a part, and apparently a considerable part, of the item "non-interest-bearing Treasury certificates," for which a single figure is given under the short-term domestic debt. From April 1, 1938, through July 31, 1938, the latest date for which official figures are available, it appears that a total of about RM1,800,000,000 delivery certificates was issued.

For the sake of completeness, I add, as part of the short-dated debt of the Reich, RM400,000,000 of treasury bills and RM1,600,000,000 of treasury certificates, both fairly constant items from one year to another, but neither playing an important part in the present reconstruction activities of the country.

Running side by side with the various forms of short-dated debt, is the new financing at long term. There were no such issues by the present regime in 1933 or 1934, but a general lowering of interest rates in the latter year prepared the ground for a long-term issue in 1935. Since then new issues have been offered fairly regularly. The latest was announced on October 1, 1938, in the sum of RM1,500,000,000, which if sold in that amount will bring the total of long-dated loans issued under the present regime to RM11,600,000,000. All bear a rate of 4½ percent and have maturities ranging from ten to twenty-seven years from the date of issue.

We now come to an interesting economic question which lies at the core of the matter we are discussing. How is it that such large public debts can be incurred, and their proceeds spent, without causing a marked and accelerating rise in the circulation of hand-to-hand currency?

Let me first give the facts on the Reichsbank's circulation, which, of course, forms the preponderant part of Germany's hand-to-hand currency.

The note circulation of the Reichsbank at the end of April, 1933, stood at RM4,022,000,000. At the end of April, 1938, the figure had risen to RM6,086,000,000, of which about RM900,000,000 was attributable to the consolidation of the former Austrian circulation with that of Germany. Thus during the first five years of National Socialist administration, the note issue of the Reichsbank, less the Austrian circulation, increased by about RM1,100,000,000, or say 25 percent. This is not an undue nor alarming increase when one considers that production rather more than doubled in the same period, and that the number of those employed increased about 55 percent. And, as we have already seen, it had no appreciable effect on the index of commodity prices and was not permitted to register its effect on the foreign exchanges.

But of course that is not the whole story. I think the dominant cause was that during the whole period the money income of the country was continuously canalized into the public hand. Tax revenues of the central and local governments progressively increased. In the fiscal year 1932–33 they stood at RM10,200,000,000. By the fiscal year 1937–38 they had risen to RM18,000,000,000. The effect of such an increase in tax revenues on the size of the circulation is all the more repressive when it is understood that in Germany income taxes are not directed at the large incomes alone, but at workmen's wages also. The day laborer and the cleaning woman pay income taxes in their degree, just as the corporation manager and the financial officer do in theirs. It is interesting to recall that the broad incidence of income taxation in Germany prevailed under the Republic, even when the Social Democrats were in power. It is no new thing under National Socialism.

Supplementing the canalization of income through taxation, there have been elaborate methods for canalizing investment funds also.

The capital market is subjected to very rigid control. Private enterprise for several years has been practically prohibited from approaching it, and only in the last twelve months or so has it been able to place relatively small issues, on the ground that these were in furtherance of the Four-Year Plan. In fact, since 1935 flotations for private industry have been less than 10 percent of total flotations. Thus for the most part the capital market has been and continues to be available almost exclusively to the Reich, for its own purposes.

On the money and capital markets all liquid funds are drawn off, with the double purpose of preparing for eventual Reich financing and to forestall possible credit expansion with inflationary consequences. On the money market this is done through the issuance of one-name bills (*Solawechsel*) by the Gold Discount Bank. As soon as there is a plethora of funds on the money market, the Gold Discount Bank sells these one-name bills to the private banks. Most of the surplus funds are thus absorbed. On the capital market the liquid funds are drawn off through the placement of Reich loans. It has been interesting to observe the relationship between outstanding one-name bills and the timing of Reich loan placements. When the amount of outstanding one-name bills has exceeded RM1,000,000,000, it has been reasonably certain that a new Reich loan would soon be announced. By the time payment on account of a Reich loan was made, the one-name bills outstanding would decline to a very small amount.

Corresponding to the restrictions on private capital issues, there are rigid restrictions also on the private use of bank credit. According to the law on the German credit system, effective January 1, 1935, the amount of credit which the commercial banks may extend to individual customers is carefully limited, and large credit lines must be reported to the banking commissioner.

Notwithstanding all the measures outlined above, the danger of inflation would have been great if steps had not been taken to make the gigantic amount of outstanding *Sonderwechsel* (special bills) as harmless as possible. When the special bills were first issued, the cash position of banking and industry was very liquid, and neither the banks, in lesser measure, nor industry, in greater measure, was averse to having these bills in their portfolios, because of the favorable return they yielded. For all realized that if they should require cash, the bills could always be discounted at the Reichsbank.

As time passed on, however, conditions changed. Further special bills were being issued in such large quantities that uneasiness was spreading as to their goodness. Added to this, industrial activity was fast increasing, and industrial enterprises were requiring not only larger amounts of cash for current business but wished to be protected for the future. In consequence, growing amounts of bills were being presented to the Reichsbank for discount. It became apparent that this practice would soon threaten to convert the bank of issue into a Reich-financing institution and would lead to currency inflation. In order to abate large further presentations of special bills to the Reichsbank, the industrial enterprises, and to a lesser extent the banks, were indirectly advised that it would be better for them to hold their special bills themselves. And wherever indirect advice failed to have the desired effect, they were told directly that the general welfare necessitated their holding them.

How the banks' portfolios of special bills have increased is indicated to some extent by the following: At the end of April, 1933, the commercial bill holdings of the Reichsbank, Gold Discount Bank, Conversion Office, state and provincial banks, Clearing Association, savings banks, five large Berlin banks, and twenty other commercial banks were RM6,300,000,000; at the end of April, 1938, RM13,500,000,000. Of course, all these commercial bills were not special bills, but we would hardly be wrong in assuming that special bills represented a substantial portion of the total.

I have indicated, in the foregoing, the steps taken by the German government to finance its vast public undertakings without incurring the usual penalty of currency inflation. The danger has been avoided, first, by restricting through persuasion and, if that failed, by direct action, the use of Reichsbank credit; secondly, by controlling the money market so that liquid funds were drawn off, made unavailable for private use, and canalized into the public hand for use when necessary to repay short-dated debt or to provide the means to convert short-dated debt into long-dated certificates or bonds; and thirdly, by heavy and universal taxation.

This discussion is lengthy, but I want to add a few lines of summary, and to give a short appraisal of the existing situation.

I said at the outset that while a boom of extraordinary size and vigor is under way in Germany, the National Socialists had set themselves the task of carrying out their stupendous program of public works without producing those signs of inflation which the people had learned most to fear. Those signs are high and rising prices, collapse of the foreign exchange value of the mark, and undue expansion of the currency. On the whole, those signs of inflation have been absent, and the efforts to that end of the National Socialist government may therefore be deemed to have been successful. In each case the methods used involved arbitrary control. They included the suppression of individual enterprise in favor of the state and for the furtherance of the purposes of the state, the diversion of the money income of the country to the prosecution of public works and the objective of rearmament, and the marshaling of the nation's labor forces to the same public ends. Without these controls, the purposes could not have been achieved. Without the National Socialist state, or some other form of authoritarian government, the whole German economic structure would surely collapse.

I have often asked the question whether the structure can continue to stand, even with the authoritarian state remaining in power. In recent weeks there have been shocks to the system which suggested that the answer might be at hand. The first, and the lesser of the two, was the short but sharp stock market crisis toward the end of August, 1938. The strictly economic explanation which seemed plausible to me was that industry and the banks were so crowded with government paper that they had to sell nongovernmental securities in order to obtain cash for pay rolls. In addition, there was a political explanation, the dawning fear of war. The second and more important shock was manifested in the currency in the second half of September, when the total of the Reichsbank's note issue, including the Austrian requirement, rose slightly above RM8,000,000,000. This rise had its counterpart in other countries party to the war crisis of those weeks, and has its principal significance here only as showing the strain that war and war financing would put upon the tenuous economic structure of Germany.

Both of these incidents illustrate the vulnerability of German finances. And yet I think—and so I have been told by American and other observers competent to draw conclusions—that as long as the authoritarian state remains in power and exercises necessary controls, nothing is apt to cause a collapse except an overwhelming need for foreign exchange or a foreign war.

I have one thing more to say and then I am through. All through this discussion I have stressed the point of controls, of the invasion of private rights for the prosecution of government purposes. For my own part, I can imagine no measure of personal security, no collective benefits, no advantages which the state can confer, no national emergency short of one involving the continued existence of the United States as a nation, which would induce me to part with the liberties so freely sacrificed to an authoritarian state.

William H. Schubart

A Discussion of Foreign Exchange and Related Problems

IN CONNECTION with the subject "Foreign Exchange and Related Problems," it has been suggested that I discuss a number of closely related topics—such as imports and exports as the backbone of exchange business, the trading of arbitrageurs and banks, practices with regard to the taking of positions in exchange, changes in the exchange business in recent years, the relative importance of commercial business, speculation and activity arising out of capital movements, the nature of exchange markets as compared with earlier years, the nature of exchange markets as compared with organized bourses, the mechanics of purchasing gold in London, how it is imported and by what steps such importations influence reserves and deposits, the service of gold in maintaining exchange stability, the operation of the control funds and the importance of gold in the work of these funds, how banks and commercial houses protect their foreign investments, the art of hedging, exchange futures, the importance of controlling forward rates in stabilizing operations, the importance of forward rates in international credit operations, the operations of official exchange control, matters touching on the operations of the funds during the recent crisis, and, of course, any considerations of a proper nature with respect to monetary controls, the future of international monetary relations, the gold standard, and so forth. Any one of these subjects might well serve as the text for five or six different papers. To discuss all of them in one will, indeed, be a trial for all of us. Nevertheless, I will do the best I can.

Before going any further, I think it is important to point out that there is no such thing as an expert in foreign exchange. We are all students, for foreign exchange and the problems related thereto are complex and ever-changing and closely related to the political developments of the day. The old rules are no longer operative, for, since the time of the World War, economic dislocation in various countries of the world has required constant change of method, and experimentation has produced exchange mechanisms never attempted before.

I shall divide this discussion into three sections. First, I shall discuss for a few minutes the definitions and mechanics of present-day exchange. Secondly, I shall touch on gold, the Tripartite Agreement, the operation of the exchange funds and the effects thereof, and lastly, the general and political aspects of foreign exchange.

SECTION 1

To start with, let us examine a classical definition of foreign exchange. Tate's *Modern Cambist* (28th edition by William S. Spalding, 1929) says: "The term foreign exchanges expresses a method by which one country discharges its liabilities to another." Under normal circumstances international trade reaches every part of the world. Countries exchange raw materials, manufactured goods, and services, tourists travel the world over and carry their money from one country to another, shipping companies of one country transport the freight of another, and many of the large insurance companies of the world insure risks for nationals of other countries, ashore and afloat. In the old days, when debt service was considered a moral obligation and people really paid the interest on their foreign loans, settlement of such interest charges was a considerable factor in the international movement of funds. Now, if we were to prepare a balance sheet of each nation, we would find that after debiting or crediting all the abovementioned items, there would remain a balance *due to* or *due from* one country to another. This is called the "Balance of Payments" and would have to be settled via the channels of foreign exchanges. If foreign exchange balances held by one country in another were insufficient, such differences would have to be settled by the transfer of gold from the debtor to the creditor country. The problem would be quite simple if it concerned two nations dealing exclusively with each other, but this is not always the case, the settlement of international balances being sometimes carried on through a great many countries before the balances are cleared. In actual practice the adjustment of the exchanges takes place daily in the open markets of the big financial centers of the world.

In the good old days, before the World War, most of the civilized countries of the world had a fixed gold standard, and the settlement of exchange differences could be accomplished without major dislocation. In those days (the United States was a debtor and not a creditor country) the experienced London market maintained balance in the exchanges through its free-gold market, by means of its export and import points, and by acting as political policeman and financial guardian of most of the trading countries of the world. She saw to it that there was a balance of political power and also that the financially weaker countries were bolstered with loans, secured from the richer countries, such operations being arranged by the thoroughly experienced private banking houses of London. She knew that to maintain her own position as a trading country and to dispose of the products of her own dominions, she had to maintain her customers solvent. In those days interest rates were effective in correcting the flow of funds from one center to another. These rates were *effective* because all funds were being used actively in industry, the development of new frontiers, and promotional enterprises of every type at home and abroad. I mention this because it is important to bear in mind that the machinery of international trade and international settlements was pretty well in balance throughout the trading countries in the years before the war, with the result that minor dislocations could be settled by adjustment of interest rates to attract or repel capital, by small amounts of gold shipped in one direction or another, or by efforts to increase exports or decrease imports. The above-mentioned machinery is largely ineffective today, for now there are huge balances of uninvested capital, idle funds whose owners are afraid to employ them in promotional or industrial enterprises, largely because of political insecurity at home, and partly because the financial reward formerly available to the successful entrepreneur has been reduced to the vanishing point. (I mention all these points to show that the classical definition of foreign exchange which I mentioned before does not entirely apply today.) Foreign exchange no longer consists of the daily balancing of trade, commercial, and other items. Today a major portion of the business consists in effecting the transfer of frightened capital as it moves from one country to another in search of security, and trade factors appear to be less and less important as the different nations of the world become increasingly self-sufficient or resort to barter.

Before going further, I should like to speak of what is meant by "future exchange contracts." If we think of foreign exchange as merchandise, then "futures" are merely memorandum contracts, by virtue of which a buyer or seller of merchandise agrees to buy or sell goods for delivery and payment at some future date.

The cotton farmer plants his seed and while his crop is still growing he may find that the price of cotton is sufficiently high to warrant him a decent profit. He therefore arranges through his cotton merchant to dispose of his cotton for forward delivery, that is, he contracts immediately to sell his cotton *when* it is prepared for market and ready for delivery, and in that way he fixes the actual amount of dollars he will receive when the cotton is ready for delivery. Having done this, he can determine fairly accurately what his profit will be and can accordingly arrange his living expenses, his expenditures for the improvement of his farm, and other related items with a considerable degree of security. Forward exchange contracts follow the same thought and mechanism. The Cuban sugar planter, in March, may contract for the sale of his raw sugar in the London market, for delivery in the late summer months or in the fall. Once his sugar has been sold abroad in terms of sterling, he knows that he will become the owner of sterling at so much per bag, the sterling coming into his possession when the sugar is delivered in London. Preferring to know exactly what he *will receive* in terms of dollars, the planter goes to his bank and sells his sterling "for future delivery" and receives from his bank a contract stating that the bank will buy from him his entire sterling proceeds, as and when received in London, agreeing to give him in exchange therefor a fixed sum of dollars representing the proceeds of the sterling. As far as the Cuban planter is concerned, his exchange risk is covered and he can eliminate this business risk from his calculations and confine himself to the problems of getting his product ready for shipment.

Let us examine another case in which future contracts are valuable to the American manufacturer. A local manufacturer of typewriters determines that he will establish an agency in London to sell his product to the English trade. He manufactures several thousand typewriters and ships them to London, where they are placed in a warehouse pending sale in the British Isles. The American manufacturer knows precisely what these typewriters cost him to manufacture and ship in terms of dollars, and he knows the exact cost of maintaining his London sales agency. He knows the price at which the typewriters are listed in terms of sterling, but he does not know how many dollars he will receive for his sterling when the typewriters are actually sold and paid for. Accordingly, he goes to his bank to chat with the head of the Foreign Exchange Department. This gentleman ascertains the total proceeds to be derived from the sale of the typewriters, the approximate time which it should take to sell them, and the cost of operating the sales agency for the given period necessary to complete the sale. Obviously, given normal conditions, the American manufacturer will be entitled to receive the gross proceeds of sale, less the cost of operating his London agency. The bank arranges to purchase from the manufacturer the net sterling proceeds of these anticipated sales and arranges for the future contracts. Since these future contracts can be adjusted at any time to suit the needs of the manufacturer, it is obvious that the latter can maintain himself in a hedged position, having only to concern himself with the business of selling the typewriters. This service is particularly valuable in these days of fluctuating exchanges, because it is often impossible for the United States manufacturer to change his list price in England when sterling declines, since his competitor, the English manufacturer of the same product, is not as closely concerned with the relation between the dollar and sterling, because in his case his proceeds are in sterling and all his costs are in sterling, and he does not gain or lose if sterling rises or falls in terms of dollars.

Now a word regarding the daily operations of a foreign exchange department. This department, in a large bank, is simply a merchandising agency which is constantly in touch with all principal foreign centers and thus is able to serve its customers by placing at their disposal the best available means of disposing of or purchasing their exchange requirements to the best possible advantage.

As soon as the market opens, cabled quotations begin to pour into the trading room from European, Canadian, and South American markets which are then open, and the operator begins his daily business by buying and selling whatever currencies his clients are interested in. He may use the facilities of the local market, because all of the principal banks are interconnected by means of brokers, and throughout the day exporters and importers all over the United States clear their requirements via the banks and transact their business in buying and selling exchange. If the dealer finds himself long or short of any particular currency, he has the option, if a counter transaction is difficult in the local market, of sending offsetting orders to his correspondents abroad, either in London, Amsterdam, or Paris, which are the principal foreign exchange markets open during our trading day.

If he is long, for instance, of £50,000, he can immediately flash a cable to one of his London correspondents to buy $250,000 at best, which, being done, flattens out his position; or he can sell, let us say, $100,000 worth of guilders, $100,000 worth of French francs, and $50,000 worth of Swiss francs, and then send cables to these foreign centers to buy an equivalent amount of these exchanges against the pound because he knows almost exactly the rate at which sterling stands in terms of all the other principal currencies, at any moment during the day, in Paris, Amsterdam, Switzerland, and London.

As a rule, large positions are not taken, because of rapidly changing tendencies which have been the rule during the last few years. Exceptions are made, however, when the foreign situation becomes such as to make it obligatory to hedge the bank's position in foreign countries to the extent that it has investments of one kind or another, such as merchandise in transit or bank balances abroad, which must always be maintained in order to provide a foreign exchange service for its many clients.

It is the opinion in many circles that a bank can operate as a commission broker in the purchase or sale of foreign exchange—in other words, that it can operate without taking even a temporary position for a few moments during the day. The New York banks give one another the most strenuous competition, and if one bank has no sterling and is required to sell to one of its customers the sum of £100,000 on a competitive basis, you may rest assured that it could not repurchase this sterling within the next few moments without paying a small premium, that is to say, without assuming a loss. In short, the foreign exchange operator has to act as a merchant. First, he must select the cheapest markets in which to buy his merchandise, and in this case it may be France, Holland, Switzerland, or England. He must act with lightning speed and, having purchased his merchandise, he must dispose of it as quickly as possible at a narrow margin of profit, for exchange profits *are* narrow. Banks often deal in $50,000 of exchange for a profit of $6.25, out of which cable charges must be defrayed.

The foreign exchange trader also acts as an arbitrageur. This word is often misused. Pure arbitrage involves a simultaneous operation over two and often three or more points. Let me describe a three-point arbitrage. Bear in mind that the foreign exchange desk is receiving from minute to minute cabled quotations of the principal exchanges coming from London, Amsterdam, and Paris markets. These cables also contain indications showing the trend, that is to say, whether an exchange is bid or offered. Let us assume for a moment that a lively foreign exchange trader notices that the French people are sellers of sterling, while at the same time the local market is buying sterling and selling francs. He immediately operates with the greatest speed. He purchases francs in his local market at what he considers a relatively low figure; simultaneously he purchases sterling in Paris, where it is offered; and at the same instant he sells sterling to eager buyers in New York. If his judgment has been good, he will have made a round trip and after his transactions are balanced off, he will show a profit in dollars. In effect, this is what he has done: he has spent, let us say, $100,000 in New York, for which he has received roughly 4,000,000 francs; with the francs he has purchased in Paris roughly £20,000; and simultaneously he has sold the same £20,000 in New York, receiving dollars in payment. He has moved

$100,000 from New York to Paris, Paris to London, and from London back to New York. When the transaction has been figured out, he may have $100,125, that is to say, a profit of $125 for his trouble, from which he has to deduct his cable expense, which in this case we may approximate at $10. To do this kind of business requires the greatest skill, for there are traders sitting in London and Paris banks, as well as in other New York banks, who are trying to seize the very same opportunity. It is this competition to take such "arbitrage profits" that keeps the currencies in parity relationship with one another. So much for the definition of arbitrageur.

SECTION 2

We have heard a good deal in recent years regarding the American Stabilization and the British Equalization Funds. First let us consider the British Fund, which anticipated its American counterpart. The Equalization Fund came into being in July, 1932, with some £25,000,000 of foreign exchange balances turned over to it by the Bank of England, and with the power to sell £150,000,000 of treasury bills. In May, 1933, its borrowing power was increased by £200,000,000 and last year a similar amount was added, so that roughly it disposes of £550,000,000, or an equivalent of $2,750,000,000.

The American Fund, which followed the devaluation of the dollar in 1934 (Gold Reserve Act, 1934), was capitalized at $2,000,000,000, earmarked out of the book profit created by devaluing the dollar. Of this large amount apparently only $200,000,000 is used for operating purposes.

The two Funds operate secretly, and little authoritative information is available as to operating methods. There are certain general conclusions that may be drawn from observation.

The British Fund was established to check violent fluctuations in the sterling-dollar rate, but it has come to serve in other directions as well. As far as possible, it acts to neutralize heavy purchases of gold and the accumulation of sterling bank deposits by outsiders. It also offsets withdrawals of banknotes for hoarding, a practice common in recent years. It has the power to sell bills to the banks, the discount market, or the Bank of England, and to sell gold to the Bank of England. Thus it can create deposits by the sale of treasury bills or by acquiring gold in the open market, or—and the converse—it can sell gold to the Bank of England and buy in its treasury bills with the proceeds. It can also sell bills to the Banking or Issue Departments of the Bank of England. Thus it can sterilize, neutralize, or insulate, whichever term you prefer, nearly any kind of inward or outward movement of capital, in whatever form this may appear. It cannot neutralize the purchase of British works of art nor castles in Scotland by Americans, but no doubt a way will soon be found.

The American Fund seems to attempt none of these operations, preferring to confine itself to the support of sterling and occasionally of francs. The Treasury attempted sterilization for a time, but apparently it is not continuing this course, preferring to permit incoming funds to have their effect in broadening our credit base.

Roughly estimated, we are said to have nearly $9,000,000,000 of foreign capital in our structure. Of this, about $3,000,000,000 are estimated as "hot money"—funds that are liquid and might be withdrawn at any time. If they are withdrawn, they will be taken in gold, so that our gold holdings of $14,000,000,000 should really be set up as two funds: one of $10,000,000,000 to $11,000,000,000 for our own purposes, while some $3,000,000,000 should be set aside as a reserve to cover loss of transient funds.

The Bank of England has not yet written into its books the gold profit which might have been obtainable had it decided to place a new gold value on its notes. There were two distinct reasons for this action: First, at that time, many English economists believed that sterling would, at a later date, return to the old gold standard and, if that had occurred, the apparent gold profit would have disappeared. After the American devaluation, it was self-evident that a return to the old gold value of the pound was out of the question. It would have meant a pound sterling having a value of about $8. Then it was reasoned that there was little sense in setting a fixed price for sterling in terms of gold, until such time as economic and political conditions in Europe and at home would enable them to set the new value with the expectation that it could remain fixed for an indefinite period of time. As political and economic conditions abroad have grown more and more complicated, it may be that the price of sterling in terms of gold may not be definitely set in our lifetime. In the American case, it was decided not to set a fixed limit for the price of gold, but instead a fixed range within which the Secretary of the Treasury, acting with the approval of the President of the United States, could determine the number of grains of fine gold contained in each United States dollar. You will remember that in 1933 and 1934 the price of one ounce of gold was raised progressively from $20.67 to the present price of $35.00. At $35.00 an ounce, the amount of gold contained in the dollar is 59.06 percent of what it contained on the old basis prior to 1933.

GOLD CONTENT PER DOLLAR

(480 Grains [troy] to the Ounce)

Price per Ounce	*Grains*	*Fine*
$20.67	25.80	9/10
	23.22	1000
$35.00	15.238	9/10
	13.714	1000

The Secretary of the Treasury and the President have the right to increase the price of an ounce of gold in terms of dollars up to $41.34 an ounce (50 percent of the previous content) or to reduce the price of an ounce of gold to approximately $34.45 (60 percent of the previous content). This right expires June 30, 1939, unless it is renewed in the meantime.[1] Put differently, the dollar may be fixed at between 50 percent and 60 percent of its old value in gold.

The French also established a Stabilization Fund, in 1936, by earmarking a portion of their devaluation profits (10,000,000,000 francs; since increased), without, however, writing down the gold value of the franc all the way to its then-current international exchange value. The French practice, from time to time, has been, in part, to support its exchange with loans made in Belgium, Switzerland, and primarily in England, using gold from the supply owned by the Bank of France as collateral for such loans. More recently, the French Fund, now operated by the Bank of France, has received advances of French francs from the treasury or from the special fund set up to stabilize French *rentes*. This prevents stabilizing operations from appearing in the statement of the Bank of France. Sales of gold, resulting in French francs deposits, are buried in the private accounts of the Bank of France and are not readily ascertainable. The French Fund is distinct from its British and American counterparts in that it does not confine itself to spot transactions; occasionally it deals largely in futures, which play a big role in French finances.

From their inception, there has been a certain degree of coöperation between the English and American Funds, for obviously it is important for them to coöperate rather than to waste their substance in opposite tactics. This led eventually to what is known as the "Tripartite Agreement." At best this is a very loose arrangement, the object of which is to check sudden and large fluctuations in the value of any two exchanges in terms of each other. Some such arrangement was badly needed, in order to promote conditions conducive to the return of international trade. If currencies had continued to fluctuate violently, export and import business would have been more seriously hampered. Perhaps it might be

[1] That power was extended to June 30, 1941, by Act of Congress approved July 6, 1939.

clearer to say that the three funds were designed to cushion the tremendous movements of capital that have become so well known in these days, and which result from political insecurity. England shipped us $641,000,000 in gold between January 1 and October 7, 1938. Obviously the Tripartite Agreement cannot undertake to fix permanently exchange prices of the currencies of the respective countries, because of the tremendous changes in the economic positions of these countries, caused by variations in the channels of trade, unemployment problems, and the heavy drain of rearmament expenditures, not to speak of war. This situation is more clearly evident in France, which has been forced successively to depreciate its exchange until today it stands at about 8 percent of its pre-war value in terms of gold, in spite of the efforts of the Funds to support it. For the purpose of this discussion, it will be sufficient to consider the British and the American Funds. In the recent crisis, when sterling was under pressure because there were hundreds of capitalists and small business men in England and on the Continent who were afraid that England might be forced into war and who consequently wished to remove their floating capital from London to New York, the British Equalization Fund sold dollars and bought sterling from the opening of business until the close of business in London, and then passed this duty on to the Federal Reserve Bank in New York, which, acting either for account of the British Fund or for the American Stabilization Fund, pursued the same tactics. As a result, sterling suffered at worst a maximum depreciation of only 5 percent, whereas, if the Funds had not been active, this temporary depreciation might have gone to 10, 15, or even 20 percent before "peace with honor" was finally achieved. Such fluctuations provide the greatest obstacle to international trade, for often commercial profit margins are wiped out by exchange losses. Besides, such violent movements cause untold problems for the responsible financial government authorities. The operation of the Funds in this crisis is typical, for while the panic in sterling was held in check, no attempt was made to restore it to the price at which it stood last summer before Hitler moved eastward. You will remember that sterling had been in the neighborhood of $4.95–$5.05 for quite a long period, and stood at approximately $4.90 some weeks before the crisis. During the ten days preceding the "Munich Accord," sterling dropped to a low of $4.61, in spite of the operations of the Fund. It was brought back to $4.84 and is currently at $4.77. The Funds have made little attempt to restore sterling to its former range, $4.95–$5.05, and they have been occupied, day by day, in stemming the current decline in the value of the pound, for until recently capital continued to move to this country in enormous volume. We will discuss the fundamental reasons for this a little later on.

Now it is timely to examine how the Funds settle their accounts with one another. When the Federal Reserve Bank, acting for the American Stabilization Fund, purchases sterling, the British Equalization Fund promptly transfers or earmarks gold in favor of the United States, on an agreed basis, to the amount of the sterling purchased by the American Fund. The American Fund then has two options—if sterling, purchased on a declining market, turns strong, the American Fund may elect to resell the sterling in London or in New York, thus taking back the dollars it had originally expended. If, however, owing to the continued weakness of sterling, this operation cannot be carried out, it may then elect to take gold, in exchange for its sterling purchases, for shipment to the United States. This has been the general practice pursued in recent months, as is apparent from the constant increase in the American holdings of gold. We have approximately $14,000,000,000 worth of gold in the United States now, and in the three weeks ending October 7, 1939, gold shipments to this country totaled roughly $430,000,000. This figure includes shipments from England, Holland, Sweden, and Canada, but the bulk of it is English gold. It is important to point out that not all of this gold is shipped because of the operations of the Stabilization Fund resulting from flight of capital—some of it undoubtedly results from substantial purchases in this country of cotton, wheat, aeroplanes, and other manufactures essential to the rearmament program.

Concerning ourselves with the mechanical aspect of these operations, let us consider for a moment how these gold shipments are handled, for they are partly the result of operations by the British and the American authorities and partly due to private shipments arranged by banking institutions here and abroad, because of the margin of profit involved therein. Formerly all gold shipments were in the hands of the private banks; today this function is being taken over more and more by the central banks, but there is still a portion of this business available to private banking institutions. American banks may buy gold abroad and bring it into this country, but they are not permitted to export gold abroad. This latter privilege is reserved exclusively to the Federal Reserve Bank, acting for the Stabilization Fund or on behalf of the United States Treasury.

Let us examine a typical gold transaction. Every morning at 11:00 A. M. in London (6:00 A. M. New York time) four bullion brokers—Samuel Montagu and Company, Mocatta and Goldsmid, Sharps and Wilkins, and Pixley and Abel—send their representatives to the office of N. M. Rothschild, who are the agents for the British Royal Mint Refinery. The house of Rothschild acts for the sellers, who are principally the gold-producing companies in South Africa, Indian potentates, or other European treasuries or firms who may elect to dispose of their bullion through the agency of this firm. A price is bid by the buyers and offered by the sellers, such price being predicated primarily on the value of gold as determined by the American Treasury price, namely $35.00 an ounce, and the current open-market price of sterling in terms of dollars. Let us assume that the pound is quoted at $5.00. As we are aware, the American price for gold is $35.00; therefore, under such conditions, an ounce of gold would fetch $35.00 in New York and, if $35.00 will produce £7 at $5.00 to the pound, then the value of an ounce of gold in London at that moment should be £7 or 140 shillings. After a few minutes of discussion, in which the determining factor is whether there is a preponderance of buyers or sellers, the price is "fixed" in the immediate vicinity of 140 shillings. If there are more sellers than buyers, the price may be just under 140 shillings, and if there are more buyers the reverse may be true. The fixing price is then applied to the majority of the transactions in gold that are to be consummated on that day, although transactions are often made at varying prices later on in the day, the controlling factor being the price of sterling. Let us suppose that the price is "fixed" at 140 shillings, and that immediately thereafter the price of sterling drops from $5.00 to $4.95. If gold can still be secured at 140 shillings per ounce, it is profitable for an American or an English bank to export a substantial quantity of gold from London to New York, for there will be a profit of five cents in the pound, that is to say of 1 percent, less all the expenses involved in the shipment. Obviously if the price of sterling declines, the price of gold will be marked up in terms of shillings and pence, but if the foreign exchange trader is quick to note such movement, he may be successful in purchasing his sterling cheaply enough to buy and ship the gold to the United States with a margin of profit to himself. The following pro-forma statement covers such a gold shipment, had it been made as of October 5, 1938, and shows the principal items of expense involved.

October 7, 1938

PRO-FORMA INVOICE COVERING SHIPMENT OF GOLD PURCHASED IN THE LONDON MARKET ON OCTOBER 4 FOR SHIPMENT PER "SS. NORMANDIE," SAILING OCTOBER 5, ARRIVING OCTOBER 10, 1938

Cost per Ounce of Gold		
$34.756491	28,771.604 fine ounces, at 145/3½d at 4.78 7/16 ($34.75649088 per oz. fine)	$1,000,000.00

.008689	Brokerage 1/4 0/00 in London	250.00 †
.000624	Cooperage in London 4/0d per box—(1,600 ounces)—18 boxes	17.94
.095580	Freight at 27½¢ per $100 (5/6d percent)	2,750.00
.038093	Insurance average rate 4.71¢ per $100 marine plus 6¼¢ per $100 war risk—10.96¢ per $100	1,096.00 ‡
.001043	Trucking New York pier to United States Assay Office, 3¢ per $1,000	30.00
.086891	Handling charge, United States Assay Office, 1/4 percent	2,500.00
.001053	Melting charge United States Assay Office, 10¢ per 100 gross ounces—about 1/33 0/00	30.30
.005793	* Estimated loss to be expected in melting 1/6 0/00 if .995 fine or better	166.67
.002896	Interest 6 days at 1/2 percent—$1,000,000	83.33 ¶
.000144	Interest 12 days at 1/2 per cent on $25,000—United States Assay Office "hold back"	4.17 ¶
$34.997297	Total cost and all expenses and interest	$1,006,928.41
$35.	Sale to United States Assay Office, 28,771.604 fine ounces at $35.00	$1,007,006.14
$ .002703	Profit over expenses and interest	$ 77.73

* If coin bars are .900 fine, the estimated loss in melting would be 1/4 0/00—an added cost of $83.33 or $0.002896 per ounce.

† This business is usually done joint account, each end taking $125.

‡ This is variable and affects shipping points.

¶ This is also part of the profit on transaction.

Gold shipments are sometimes made to sell sterling (by shipping gold and receiving dollars).

The final step to be discussed here concerns the absorption of the arriving gold by the United States Treasury Department. (I speak in this case of an importation arranged by the Federal reserve bank; in the final analysis, however, importations arranged by private banks bring about the same results, although the initial steps may vary.) The gold upon its arrival will be deposited in the New York Assay Office, under supervision of representatives of the Federal reserve bank. The Assay Office will deliver to the Federal reserve bank a United States Treasury check in payment of the gold. Obviously the Treasury Department may wish to replenish its account for the sum laid out for the purchase of the gold. This is accomplished as follows: The Treasury Department will issue gold certificates for the exact amount of the gold purchased and will deposit these gold certificates in the Federal Reserve Board Clearance Fund for account of the New York Federal Reserve Bank. The latter will credit the Treasury on its books for an amount equivalent to the gold certificates issued to it. You will note that the original expenditure of dollars by the American Stabilization Fund has now been reimbursed by a payment from the United States Treasury, while the Treasury has replenished its own account through the issue of gold certificates into the Federal Reserve System. As a result of this operation, there has been a gain in deposits of the member banks exactly equivalent to the amount of gold imported. Unless there is an extraordinary increase in business activity calling for additional currency, there is an immediate increase in the reserves of member banks held by the Federal Reserve Bank. The increased deposit liability requires an increase in required reserves, but the balance over and beyond said required reserve becomes idle funds, known as excess reserves. Currently there are such idle or excess reserves in the Federal Reserve System to the credit of member banks, in an amount in excess of $3,000,000,000, and these funds will be increased as more and more gold is shipped into the country, unless there is an increase of bank loans. In order to avoid this increase in excess reserves (idle money), the basis of what is sometimes called fountain-pen money, the Treasury can sterilize the incoming gold shipments, as it has done in the past. This is accomplished very simply: the Treasury purchases the gold, but instead of issuing gold certificates to reimburse itself, it sells Treasury bills to the member banks or to the public, thus merely shifting deposits and preventing an increase in excess reserves. The disadvantage of the latter method lies in the fact that, under conditions similar to those existing now, the government interest-bearing debt would be substantially increased. Incidentally, it is important to point out that the attitude of the Treasury as to whether it should sterilize or issue gold certificates is largely dependent upon its open-market policy, as well as upon other current factors. At the present time the policy may be described as inflationary, for the present gold influx is being put back into the system so that the glut of idle money becomes greater and greater. Obviously, the authorities are hoping in this way to push money into industry, and incidentally to support the weakened commodity structure as far as it is possible to do so.

SECTION 3

It might be fair to say that the foreign exchange problem lies at the root of the present political crisis in Europe, a crisis that has been developing ever since the end of the World War. By depriving it of its colonies, and by subjecting it to heavy financial penalties, the Allies dismembered the economic machinery of Germany. At the moment we are not considering the moral issues involved. In an effort to pay her debts and to reconstruct herself after the war and indirectly to make indemnity payments, Germany incurred huge new foreign obligations by borrowing from different countries of the world. When this debt was called for payment in 1929 and 1930, Germany had neither a sufficiently large balance of trade in her favor nor enough foreign exchange or gold to enable her to meet her creditors, and we are fully aware of the different events that led to the moratorium in 1931. Having lost certain of her important sources of raw materials, and having no assets on hand with which to purchase such requirements, Germany had to resort to barter and to seek self-sufficiency by artificial substitutes. This difficult period in German economic history can be explained in one short sentence—Germany had no foreign exchange and was left no way of creating it—result: a desire for self-sufficiency, and, when even that effort did not provide the expected results, it concluded that there remained but one way open, namely, the occupation of territory from which it could derive the materials necessary for a rounded economy. Put differently, I doubt whether Germany would have developed its present political philosophy had there been sufficient foreign exchange available to it to supply its needs. It is well within the range of possibility that Czechoslovakia might today be intact, and Germany might still have a Republican form of government, if the rest of the world had been willing to accept freely German export goods in trade for copper, nickel, oil, rubber, coffee, and tea. The economic dislocation which was brought on by the Treaty of Versailles was by no means confined to Germany, for it also brought about dangerous unbalance in Central Europe. It was in Austria that the disease first had its effect, in the failure of the Credit-Anstalt. In Italy the lack of purchasing power abroad was an important factor in the development of fascism, and the need for raw materials undoubtedly was one of the reasons for the Ethiopian affair, which was the forerunner of the recent German program of forced *Anschluss*. Had there been men of great wisdom and foresight, long-term international loans to Germany, Austria, and Italy might have forestalled the present-day need for rearmament, with all the waste of money and the threat of war that such a program carries with it. If in the twenties public opinion could have been educated to the dangers involved in the then-existing economic theory, the world might have been a different place to live in now. At the present moment rearmament is bleeding the French economic system to the point where it is within the range of possibility that the French franc may lose all its value and a new currency system be needed. England is facing a similar problem, for, with a negative trade balance and a diminishing income from colonial and foreign investments, it also has many dangerous years ahead. It is logical to say that if the "have" countries do not purchase the exports of the "have-not" countries and refuse them loans, then, in the long run, the "have" countries will have no customers left.

Of the gold held by the United States, France, and Britain, we have about 80 percent. As the political situation of Great Britain becomes more difficult, capitalists large and small the world over may continue to send their accumulated balances from London to New York. Under existing conditions, this can be accomplished only by further heavy shipments of gold. If we permit the other countries of the world to be drained of their gold, and if at the same time we refuse to take their goods, international trade will gradually disappear and only barter can take its place.

England has certain great advantages, in that it has an incalculable supply of gold available in South Africa and in Canada and, barring the severest conditions, may be able to import sufficient gold for its own purposes. This will involve the sale of sufficient manufactures to Canada and South Africa to enable it to take in gold at the same rate of speed at which it loses it to the United States. The strain upon England will be severest during the process of transferring idle capital from London to New York. Once this process is completed, England should lose gold to us only to the extent that it requires American raw materials or manufactures.

The obvious solution is the redistribution of our own gold among the nations of the world that trade with us. It is equally obvious that we cannot do this unless we have some assurances that we will be repaid in time, and that there is a solid foundation for peace in the world.

Question has arisen as to whether this country will further devalue the dollar. This question is, of course, impossible to answer, but to my mind such action, under present conditions, would merely hasten the day of reckoning. Prices in this country have remained relatively stable for a considerable period of time, and it is not conceivable that a further reduction in the gold value of the dollar would bring about a permanent rise in prices, any more than it did in 1934. Assuming that a given pair of shoes has had a value of $5.00 over the last five years, it is obvious that an ounce of gold shipped from Europe to America could have been converted into four pairs of shoes, with gold at $20.67 an ounce. When the price of gold was raised to $35.00 an ounce, these European countries could have secured seven pairs of shoes for the same ounce of gold, and this increase in the purchasing power of foreign gold was partly responsible for the recent tremendous influx of the metal, for our goods were cheap in terms of gold. If now we were to raise the price of gold to $40.00 or $50.00 an ounce, the same European ounce of gold would purchase eight or ten pairs of the $5.00-shoes, and this would undoubtedly result in a further drain of gold from the countries that should keep the metal. If we continue to depreciate the value of the dollar and to increase the price of gold, we will surely help to bankrupt our foreign friends and force them to find some other monetary base on which to operate their currency systems. This leaves us on the horns of a dilemma, which I shall leave to you for solution.

Carl S. Shoup

Fiscal Aspects of Old Age Reserves

THE PROBLEM of old age reserves has been the cause of much misunderstanding, owing to certain verbal difficulties. Consequently, I propose first to try to elucidate the terms involved.

I may first note that the old age system embodied in the law consists of two parts. One part concerns those persons who are employed in industry and trade, under the benefit system. The other part refers to those who are in the uncovered employments, those who are self-employed, and those who are unemployed. Persons in this second group, if they are needy when old age arrives, will receive assistance payments, varying greatly in amount from state to state. The benefit payments, on the other hand, will be made whether or not the receivers are needy, and the payments will come from Federal Government. The needy aged get their money from the state governments, but the state governments are reimbursed for approximately one-half of what they spend; that is, the Federal Government matches the state government dollar for dollar, but only up to the sum of thirty dollars per month per individual.

We can therefore distinguish between "benefits" and "assistance," between the needy and the non-needy, between the covered employments and the non-covered employments.

Let us consider some of the possible meanings of the term "reserve." One way in which it is sometimes used is to indicate the liability incurred by the government—the commitment it has made by its promise to pay old age benefits, in accordance with a specified schedule, and regardless of whether pay-roll taxes are imposed. In this sense the reserve is simply a statement of the present value of the liability incurred. This concept, however, is not that which I have in mind, in my use of the term.

There is a second way in which the reserve idea may be used. As the employer pays his pay-roll tax money to the government, he may reasonably consider that it is accumulating as a reserve, without asking what form the accumulation takes, or how it is linked with the rest of the fiscal system. This use of the term reserve concerns simply the pay-roll tax. I shall not discuss this concept of reserve, since the current discussion on the reserve problem will clearly include points involving the whole fiscal system.

The third meaning of the term is that of a fiscal-system reserve. Under this concept, in order to discover whether a reserve is being created, it is necessary to look at the fiscal system as a whole. If, as soon as this money is paid to the government, the government spends it, then as far as the fiscal system as a whole is concerned, no reserve is being built up. The inflow of the money is being counterbalanced by an expenditure (which would not otherwise have been made).

A fourth possible definition of the term reserve is that of an economic reserve. Here the question is: does the collection of the pay-roll taxes now make it any easier for the taxpayers of later years? Is there any transfer of the burden of taxation from one generation to another?

A fiscal-system reserve exists (1) when the government has been committed to a series of expenditures that can reasonably be forecast, and (2) when the net tax increase paid in, in order to cover these expenditures, comes earlier than these expenditures. The reserve may be called a full or complete reserve if the net tax increase is large enough and comes early enough so that the interest on this increase, plus the then current pay-roll taxes, will cover the payments to the aged in the years when these payments are assumed to stabilize. Any net tax increase short of that will create a reserve that cannot last. In that case the government will have to contribute from general revenues either to maintain the reserve or to supplement (and in time entirely replace) the interest on the reserve. But in so far as there is any fiscal-system reserve at all, the net result of the program is, of course, to reduce the amount of the public debt outstanding in private hands, as compared with what it would otherwise be. If, however, current expenditures are increased, as compared with what they would have been if no such net tax increase had been enacted, then to that extent the fiscal-system reserve fails to materialize.

Only the first two of the four reserve conceptions listed above necessarily imply the existence of a contributory feature in the old-age program (and even the first may not do so). It is possible to have a contributory system and not to have any fiscal-reserve system; that is, there may be no net tax increase in the system as a whole. For instance, some other tax may be decreased, or some expenditures increased, because of the introduction of the contributory pay-roll taxes.

There are thus four possible extreme types of systems, if we use reserve in the fiscal-system sense: a contributory reserve system; a non-contributory reserve system; a contributory non-reserve system; and a non-contributory non-reserve system. Which of these four extremes is closest to the present system of old-age benefits? The same question may be asked concerning the benefit system and the assistance system, considered as a unit.

The Social Security Act, for old age purposes, levies a pay-roll tax on employees and on employers. The pay-roll tax at the present time is one percent on employees and one percent on employers. It is scheduled to be increased so that its maximum will be 3 percent on employees and 3 percent on employers.

A certain formula determines the amount of monthly benefit the employees will get: one-half of one percent on the first $3,000 that he has earned in covered employment; plus one-twelfth of one percent of the next $42,000; plus one-twenty-fourth of one percent of all earnings over $45,000. This is called a "bent formula"; there is a bonus at the bottom of the scale, in the sense that the taxes paid by employees plus the taxes paid by employers on the first $3,000 of covered-employment earnings give a very handsome return. A by-product of this feature may be illustrated by a farmer who works in a covered occupation, let us say in an industrial establishment, for a relatively short time, earning only $3,000. The absolute amount of his old-age payment is not large, but the percentage return on it is high. This has important implications for the reserve system. The farmer in this case is, on balance, depleting the reserve. There are enough cases of this kind so that it appears that the original estimate of a $47,000,000,000 reserve may have to be cut in half. Moreover, since this fact means that the present benefit system is not a full nor complete fiscal-reserve system, the prospect is that there will be a substantial fiscal-system reserve that will reach a peak and thereafter be drained steadily until it falls to zero. Hence the present old age benefit system is not a fully contributory system, if only because of the in-and-outers who will never pay their way and because of others who will come from uncovered employments into the covered employments late in their earning life; nor is this system on a complete fiscal-system reserve basis.

Is the old age system as a whole, including the assistance part of it, on a reserve basis, on a no-reserve basis, or on a negative reserve basis (fiscal-system reserve)? This leads to the question whether present assistance payments are being met by new tax money. There is some indication that this is the case, so far as the states are concerned; but it may be doubted whether the Federal Government has increased its taxes because it has joined in this assistance program, or whether such increases as have been made have been commensurate with the assistance program. Instead, it appears that the Federal Government is increasing the privately held public debt, as a result of its part in this old age assistance system. Therefore, considering the benefit system and the assistance system together, the present old age system as a whole is closer to a no-reserve basis than to a full reserve basis (still speaking of a fiscal-system reserve).

What kind of system do we want? Do we want a fully contributory system, in the sense that each person pays to the government the actuarial equivalent of what he gets? That is not my topic of discussion, but in passing it may be noted that there are some people from whom it is not possible to get such a contribution; they do not have the economic power to give it. Do we want a fiscal-system reserve? That question can be answered only in the light of knowledge regarding the system as a whole and regarding the general state of the finances, and from this point of view such reserve may well be considered desirable. If no such attempt is made to reduce the privately held public debt [1] (compared to what it otherwise would be), when 1980 comes the country may be faced with the problem that the then-current tax requirements for debt service, plus old-age payments, will be so large that the tax system as a whole will have too-undesirable effects in checking production or in other ways. One offsetting consideration is that if the pay-roll tax proceeds are invested advantageously, future generations will have their burdens lightened, even though a fiscal-system reserve may not have been built up, while the strain caused by the large aggregate of taxation in the future may be correspondingly reduced.

[1] That is, all debt except that held by the government itself in the old-age reserve fund.

Frank D. Graham

The One-Hundred Percent Reserve System

NEARLY a century ago Samuel Jones Lloyd who, I believe, later became Lord Overstone, of the Bank of England, suggested that the business of issuing circulating medium should be separated from the business of banking. Lord Overstone was not a brilliant individual, but he was correct in this view and he was influential. The result was the Bank Act of 1844, in which England took away from the banks the power of creating tangible money. This power was removed not only from the commercial banks, but from the Bank of England itself. There was to be no further issues of notes except in so far as they were backed 100 percent by gold.

Fullarton had pointed out that bank notes were then only the small change of credit. He saw that bank notes were to demand deposits merely what subsidiary coinage was to the ordinary bank note. Lloyd did not see that at all. He was of the type who thought that the banks could not create circulating medium. It was his intention to take away from the banks all power of issuing circulating medium and to leave them only the power to lend money; but, in his failure to grasp Fullarton's point, he attained not the substance but a shadow. Fullarton represented the banking principle and Lloyd the currency principle. The controversy between the two schools is, of course, familiar to all.

The banking school was wrong in supposing that there could not be any overissue so long as the banks were held to redemption. Under the operation of the banking principle, there was the probability that the banks would issue more money than they could keep in circulation. But whether they did this or not, there was a tendency toward a cumulative process of inflation, on the basis of fractional reserves at a progressively declining ratio.

In this country—and the condition of this country in that respect is merely parallel to that of other countries—we have had a steady growth of the use of bank debt as money. In the early years of banking in this country the ratio of capital (which was *mainly* in cash) to the liabilities of banks was very high. In the first years under the National Bank Act it was around 70 to 75 percent. From this there was a steady drop until capital funds fell to 20 percent, and even lower. That situation could occur only because people got into the habit of holding bank deposits as money.

It is my feeling that there is no real distinction between bank deposits as money and any other type of money. There is a good deal said about the difference between deposits, or between a check which is a method of transferring deposits, and other forms of money. I feel that the scrutiny which we give to a check is precisely of the same character as that which we give to a bank note. A cautious individual will look at a bank note, or government money, to see that it is not counterfeit. We do no more, and no less, with a check. I look upon bank deposits unreservedly as money, and I would say that they *are* money, inasmuch as we accept a transfer of a deposit in a bank as definitive payment of any obligation that happens to be owing to us. That seems to me to constitute money; we do not draw out much cash; deposits are circulated among the banks, at the behest of individuals, precisely as ordinary money circulates in the community.

The proposal of a 100-percent reserve means that demand deposits should be backed 100 percent in cash; the two kinds of money would be merely alternative forms. In so far as one had demand deposits, the banks would be under obligation to lay aside, and physically withdraw from circulation, an equivalent amount in cash. The deposit and the cash would be interchangeable and there could not be any more of demand deposits than there would be of tangible money. Only a part of the cash, of course, would be held against the deposits. The total cash would be equal to the sum of our present demand deposits and our present cash.

Burgess points out that we have two kinds of money: high-powered and low-powered money. By high-powered money, he means tangible cash and deposits in the Federal Reserve Banks—that is to say, anything that we might designate as Federal funds. Of course the reason he calls that sort of thing high-powered money is that it allows for an expansion of low-powered money. I think that that is a useful distinction and that we ought to carry it a little further. High-powered money is an entirely different sort of thing from low-powered money. We recognize that fact when we are willing to pay more for high-powered money than for low-powered. There is the case of the bank which borrowed from the Federal Reserve Bank at 87½ percent interest—it was a country bank lending at 7 or 8 percent. It could multiply its loan from the Federal Reserve Bank about fourteen times and it was merely covering its impaired reserve ratio without any net cost. Here was a bank willing to pay 87½ percent to get high-powered money, in order to lend many times as much low-powered money, and its action was justifiable on business grounds.

This high-powered money is fertile in a sense that low-powered money is not, and I would like to raise the question whether we ought to have these different kinds of money. A 100-percent reserve, as proposed, would remove the spawning character of high-powered money and make all money of the same character. I would make the assertion that we have now reached a position in which we have almost no control over the volume of high-powered money, so long as we preserve our present monetary standard, and that this situation is highly explosive. Excess reserves are likely to continue to grow, unless or until we have the kind of inflation which would eliminate the excess reserves by piling up the volume of low-powered money. It is to that point that I want particularly to address myself. I am trying to develop the relation of our present monetary system to the control of the volume of the circulating medium.

I am inclined to think that we will eventually get all of the world's supply of gold. Why should we not? Dollars are now as good as gold to anyone, unless we do one or both of two things: (1) again raise the buying price of gold, or (2) refuse to export gold. But it does not seem to me that we will do either of these things. If we are not going to indulge in either of these follies, dollars are as good as gold can possibly be and they may be a lot better. Unless we do one of these two things gold cannot rise higher in real value than the dollar. If dollars are as good to anyone as gold, why should anyone want to hold gold? There is no inherent reason for supposing that gold will ever move outward in any large volume. We are the only country in the world which will take gold freely; it is open to any other country, except Belgium, to refuse to take gold. When other countries send gold to us, that tends to drive down the exchange value of the dollar. But this does not take gold away from us, since all that then happens is a reduction in the foreign buying price of gold sufficient to keep the foreign monetary authorities out of the market. I seriously believe, therefore, that we are likely to get the world's supply of gold. The tendency is likely to be strengthened by an armament race in Europe. Gold might be a material for war if it could be used for buying goods when war starts, but no one can be sure of being able to do that. Therefore other countries would rather have the goods now and give us the gold. Eventually, as we get more and more gold, we shall get into a situation in which there will be no control of credit supply. The gold is high-powered money and offers the possibility of expansion which is the property of that sort of money.

Perhaps that is enough to say about gold. Let us now turn to silver. We are buying silver practically in the same way as we are buying gold. There is practically free purchase of silver at a fixed price. The reasons for buying silver are even less compelling than those for buying gold. Buying silver gives us high-powered money quite as readily as buying gold does, since our purchases of silver increase the supply of tangible money. The high-powered money in bank reserves would have greatly increased if it had not been for the fact that money in circulation is rising. If the tangible money in circulation should fall, the silver certificates would simply drive the Federal Reserve notes back into the banks, to be deposited in the Reserve Banks and thus increase the reserve ratios.

The third factor making for high-powered money is the purchase of securities by the Reserve Banks. That is presumably under some control, and I will not go into the question more deeply. But the matter of gold and silver is not under the control of the reserve banks, and, on the contraction side, elasticity is therefore sadly lacking.

I think that in advocating 100-percent money, I would put it on the ground that we have these highly explosive possibilities in our present system. There is no possibility of control except by moving toward the 100-percent system and thus raising the reserve ratios above the present legal limits. New legislation, which would authorize new and increased reserve ratios, would have to be passed. One other thing which operates to reduce the explosive possibilities of our present system, it seems to me, is the practice of banks in charging for handling accounts. This charging for the handling of deposit accounts, which is a feature of the 100-percent reserve system, results in an increase in the use of cash. It is now holding down deposit balances and is resulting in a reduction of reserves in order to get cash for circulation. Even now, therefore, we have a movement toward a 100-percent reserve system.

I propose now to consider what seems to me to be an argument for 100-percent reserve on the basis of equity. As I see it, the issue of the money supply must be a monopoly of some sort. The social interest is by no means necessarily advanced by an increase in the supply of money. Therefore we must make a monopoly of it. My feeling is that if we have to have a monopoly, it ought to be a monopoly in governmental hands. Otherwise we are allowing private institutions seigniorage, which has always been held to be a government prerogative. The fact is that the banks do have seigniorage on the issue of new commercial credit. While they have 100-percent seigniorage in this respect, their expenses have been raised so much that most of this gain is paid out again. Therefore this matter of equity is probably not of very great consequence.

I think the position of the commercial banks would be somewhat improved by the adoption of the 100-percent system, in that profits would be more stable than they are now. Banks are likely to make high profits in an era when total demand deposits are increasing. On the other hand, if demand deposits are not increasing, or if they are diminishing, the banks are subjected to diminution of gross earnings, to great losses, or to both. The stability of earnings which, I think, would accompany the 100-percent reserve system, would be in the interest of the banks. I am not so enthusiastic as Fisher for 100-percent money, but I do think it would make for some degree of stability in the earnings of the banks; and I think that the average earnings, if the system were inaugurated along the lines that are desirable, would be as high as they are now as well as much more stable.

If we had the 100-percent system it would be desirable that the ownership of the Federal Reserve Banks should be vested in the government, that the Reserve Banks should then have the power to expand or to contract the circulating medium, and that no one else should have that power. The Federal Reserve Banks now have some securities, to the value of about $2,500,000,000, which could be sold to contract credit, although that seems to me wholly inadequate in that connection. I think, too, that the government has been placed in a wholly anomalous position, for it has sold bonds to the banks which the latter paid for merely by increasing deposit credits. The upshot is that the government, far from enjoying seigniorage, has been put in the position of paying banks for issuing that sort of money. That looks, on the whole, to be rather a stupid proceeding.

I want to describe briefly the present situation and to suggest how a 100-percent reserve system might be inaugurated comparatively painlessly. The demand deposits in commercial bank members of the Federal Reserve System total, in round numbers, about \$21,000,000,000. The total cash reserves are about \$8,000,000,000; in addition to that, there is some cash in till money, and so forth—say about \$1,000,000,000—or about \$9,000,000,000 altogether. The value of the government securities held by these banks is about \$12,000,000,000 to \$13,000,000,000; hence it so happens that the cash, plus the government securities held by the banks, about equals the volume of demand deposits. That suggests that we might do something along the lines laid down in the National Bank Act.

I would think that it might be done somewhat in this way: Every bank has a certain amount of cash. In some cases, such as those of central reserve city banks, the required ratio is about 22½ percent. This cash might be put against the reserve, to be applied under the 100-percent reserve system, and the rest made up by the deposit of the government bonds.

In order to give the banks the revenues which they now get, to cover the costs of helping to carry on the bookkeeping of the nation in check and deposit systems, they might be given low-interest-bearing securities in exchange for their present holdings, which would be deposited in a reserve account. The banks are now holding a great volume of government securities at practically no interest. Suppose the government were to offer, let us say, 1½ percent bonds, which could be purchased with the cash or the government bonds now on hand, to be handed over to the Federal Reserve

System as trustee, with title to be held by the commercial banks, and interest pooled. Some banks, short of cash or government securities, might be loaned these special government bonds, on any satisfactory security they chose to put up. The banks could be given the excess of the interest on their collateral over the 1½ percent which would go into the pool.

I think we could readily establish a 100-percent reserve against demand deposits in the way stated above. If any bank's deposits should decline, it would naturally want to draw out cash. The title to the special bond would then pass to the Federal Reserve Bank, which could dispose of it to banks whose deposits were increasing. It would thus go back to the pool. Commercial banks would then be placed in the same position as savings banks, with the difference merely that the savings banks would deal in long-term loans and the commercial banks in short. The possibilities of expansion arising from lack of control over new supplies of primary money would then be reduced to a 1:1 ratio, and we could look on the current and prospective expansion of reserves with some equanimity.

Daniel W. Bell

The Functions of the Bureau Of the Budget

IN DISCUSSING the present functions of the Bureau of the Budget, it might be of interest to have a picture of the system, or lack of system, which prevailed prior to 1921, when the Budget and Accounting Act became law.

The budget does not seem to have been a matter of any concern to the framers of the Constitution of the United States. They apparently accepted it on the basis of the English practice and regarded budgetary procedure as something which would take care of itself as soon as the new government had been established. When framed, the Constitution therefore carried only a brief provision relative to procedure, as follows:

> No money shall be drawn from the Treasury but in consequence of appropriations made by law; and a regular statement and account of the receipts and expenditures of all public money shall be published from time to time.

The original duties of the Secretary of the Treasury were evidently modeled upon English law and procedure. The Act of September 2, 1789, "To establish the Treasury Department," made it the duty of the Secretary "to prepare and report estimates of the public revenue and public expenditures." This act was followed by the Act of May 10, 1800, which imposed upon the Secretary the duty of digesting, preparing, and laying before Congress at the commencement of every session a report "on the subject of finance, containing estimates of the public revenue and public expenditures, and plans for improving and increasing the revenues from time to time, for the purpose of giving information to Congress in adopting modes of raising the money requisite to meeting the public expenditures." The organic law evidently contemplated that a definite budget should be submitted each year by the Secretary, as finance minister of the administration. This intention, however, was not realized. Hamilton, the first Secretary of the Treasury, submitted in person bold financial plans to the Congress. The apparent duty of the Secretary as originally contemplated was soon changed, because of jealousy and hostility engendered between the legislative and the executive branches of the government. Congress first encouraged, and then later directed by statute in certain cases, the decentralization of budgetary matters. Prior to the enactment of the Budget and Accounting Act of 1921, the statutory powers of the Secretary of the Treasury were gradually reduced, through a series of statutory provisions, from those of a "finance minister" to a mere editor without discretion.

By 1910 the financial methods of the national government had become so obviously defective and so open to political abuses that steps were taken to correct them. In this year President Taft appointed a Commission on Economy and Efficiency. After a searching investigation, covering two years, this commission made several reports setting forth its findings, the most important of which was the one entitled "The Need for a National Budget," which the President transmitted to Congress with his endorsement. He believed so strongly in the main recommendation of this report, namely, the formulation of the budget by the President, that he actually prepared "A Budget for the Fiscal Year 1914" and submitted it to Congress. But it was coldly received and practically ignored.

Although the work of the Taft Commission was neglected by Congress for the time being, it had an immediate and telling effect on the state governments. The work of the commission sufficed to provide the initial impetus toward a country-wide movement for budgetary reform among the states. Within a decade nearly every state government had provided for budgetary methods. These state experiments in budgeting were in the nature of laboratory tests, which served to demonstrate the great need for a budget system in the national government. Following the close of the World War, there was a strong popular demand for national budgetary reform, so much so that Congress could not delay the matter any longer. After extended hearings and debate, Congress finally passed a bill in June, 1920, but President Wilson vetoed this bill because of a certain restriction on his Constitutional prerogative. The next Congress passed almost an identical bill and it was signed by President Harding on June 10, 1921.

Up to this time the estimates of appropriations to carry on the activities of the government were made up independently in the various bureaus of the departments. They were then sent without revision by the head of the department to the Treasury, the Treasury exercising the purely mechanical function of assembling the estimates and transmitting them to the Congress. It can be seen that they were not at any time examined nor revised by the Chief Executive; that as thus unrevised, and without coördination as between bureaus of a department, or of a department with another department, or of proposed expenditure with estimated revenue, and without any financial statement, or budget message, or comparative tables, they did not in any sense represent a real financial or budget plan; that instead they constituted bureau-serving material which might be ignored or utilized by the Congress as it saw fit; and that in effect the legislative branch, and not the executive branch, actually prepared, in its various appropriations measures, the financial plan or budget of the central government. The Act of 1921 materially changed the old procedures.

Most writers refer to three principal steps in budgeting, namely,

(1) preparation; (2) ratification; and (3) execution. We may add a fourth—auditing.

Preparation. The Budget and Accounting Act of 1921 requires the President to transmit to the Congress a budget for each fiscal year. The law requires that it be submitted to the Congress on the first day of each regular session. In other words, the budget for the fiscal year 1940 (beginning July 1, 1939, and ending June 30, 1940), was sent to the Congress under date of January 3, 1939. As the departments are required to submit estimates of their requirements to the Budget Bureau not later than September 15, this gives the Bureau about three and a half months in which to prepare the Budget document.

After the estimates are received from the various departments, they are referred to the assistants in the bureau in charge of such departments. Here the estimates, together with the written justification which is required in each case by our regulations, are carefully studied and analyzed by the assistant in charge and two investigators, preparatory to a hearing between these Budget Bureau representatives, constituting a Hearing Committee, and those from the department concerned who have been designated to defend such estimates. These hearings last from 9:30 A. M. until about 1:00 P. M., or until the day's schedule is finished. The afternoon is usually taken up by the Hearing Committee in executive session, in order to determine what action it will recommend to the Review Committee (Director, Assistant Director, Executive Assistant, the Fiscal Assistant, and the Assistant in charge of Coordination). The assistant in charge of the department whose estimates are being considered must appear before the Review Committee and give the department's reasons for the request and his committee's reasons for its recommendation. The Director's decision is, of course, final as far as the Bureau is concerned, but he must make his recommendations to the President and obtain his approval before the estimate of appropriation can be included in the Budget. It usually takes about six weeks to compile and print the tables and statements, including the Budget Message, which constitute the Budget document.

The question may well be asked just what is accomplished by all this procedure. Let me give the results of our attempts to save the taxpayers' money during the past four years. For the fiscal year 1936 we reduced the departmental estimates by about $443,-000,000; in 1937 by $1,098,000,000; in 1938 by $775,000,000; and in 1939 by $905,000,000. By contrast, the total expenses of the Bureau, including the cost of printing the Budget document, aggregated only about $200,000 per annum as an average over the past fifteen years.

Ratification.—Ratification or enactment of the budget or financial plan is with us, as in other countries, the function of the legislative branch. Prior to 1921, however, it was unlike that of any other country. In Congress there was the same lack of coordination in handling the estimates when received as occurred in the making up of the estimates that came from the executive departments. The appropriation bills that constituted the budget or financial program were prepared by committees—ten in the House and eight in the Senate—working independently of one another and without centralized consideration on the merit of the financial proposals of the different departments of the government, or without any knowledge of the revenue expected to be received by the Treasury. But upon passage of the Budget and Accounting Act, Congress did a little reorganizing of its own. It combined all of the various appropriation committees into one committee for each House. These committees were broken up into sub-committees, such as the Sub-Committee on Treasury-Post Office Appropriation Bills, the Sub-Committee on War Department Appropriation Bills—military and non-military, and so on. The various committees hold hearings with departmental representatives and outside interested persons on the estimates of appropriations contained in the Budget document or in supplemental and deficiency submissions. The Bureau of the Budget seldom participates in these hearings. While the departmental representatives who appear before the committees may not volunteer suggestions of increases beyond the amounts of the Budget estimates, they may, upon the direct request of a committee, or one of its members, supply information favorable to such increases; and when given that opportunity they seldom fail to avail themselves of it. The other witnesses at these hearings are members of Congress who are usually seeking increases in Budget amounts or the insertion of items that have not been included in the Budget, and private individuals who invariably have the same purpose to accomplish.

It is here that the Budget faces the powerful assaults of the so-called pressure groups that are seeking new or increased appropriations for their particular projects—assaults that continue, under skilled leadership in and out of Congress, as long as the appropriation measures are under consideration in the different legislative stages through which they pass.

For example: The printed hearings of the Sub-Committee of the House Appropriations Committee considering the Department of Agriculture appropriation bill for the fiscal year 1938 contained 375 pages devoted to arguments for increased appropriations, which were made by persons other than those representing the department. Thirty-one non-governmental organizations were represented, in addition to 73 members of both bodies of Congress.

So many non-departmental representatives appeared before the House sub-committee handling the Department of the Interior appropriation bill for the fiscal year 1938 that it became necessary to publish a separate volume to cover their testimony. This separate volume of 469 pages contained the arguments for increased appropriations of 84 members of Congress and of the one or more representatives of 21 different associations and organization groups, affording stiff opposition to any budget director.

Execution.—The execution of the Budget lies with the executive branch of the government, although the legislative is very much interested in this phase of budgeting, and usually checks the executive branch through its auditing office. When the appropriation bills have passed the Congress and received the approval of the President, the funds therein appropriated are available, on the date indicated in each act, to the various departments for obligation. In other words, the departments may then begin to carry out their plans to expend the funds for the purposes and in the manner set forth in the appropriation acts under each title.

Congress has from time to time passed laws to curb deficiency appropriations, but our government is too complicated a piece of machinery for us to foresee all of the emergencies and contingencies which may arise during a year, requiring additional or new funds. In 1905 Congress passed the so-called Anti-Deficiency Act, in which it sought to curb deficiency appropriations by a method of apportionment of appropriations at such a monthly or other periodical rate of obligation as would enable each department to end the fiscal year within the amount of its appropriation.

The apportionments of appropriations under the Anti-Deficiency Act were originally under the sole control and guardianship of the heads of departments and establishments, and their purpose was that of avoiding the incurrence of deficiencies. But with the enactment of the Budget and Accounting Act of 1921, and, in particular, through the provisions of an Executive Order issued by President Roosevelt under reorganization authority of 1933, the control of apportionments has passed to the Bureau of the Budget, and it has been set up there as a measure, not only for the avoidance of deficiencies but for the accomplishment, when possible, of savings through the establishment of reserves at the beginning of the fiscal year. The reserves are released only upon a proper showing that the funds are necessary in the conduct of the government business. Let us glance at what has been accomplished in the way of savings, during the past four years, through the operation of reserves. At the beginning of the fiscal year 1936, we set up reserves aggregating $224,000,000, of which $138,000,000 were released during the year, thus saving $86,000,000. In 1937 we set up reserves aggregating $234,000,000, of which $68,000,000 were released and $166,000,000 saved. In 1938 we set up $472,000,000 and released $228,000,000, thus saving $244,000,000; and in 1939 we set up $303,000,000 and have released to date $48,000,000. We hope the balance of $255,000,000, or the greater part of it, can be saved. Generally speaking, the record has improved, but of course the total appropriations upon which we base our reserves have grown broader during the past few years.

It is necessary for us to keep in close touch with every phase of government activity so as to be able to make as intelligent a decision as possible, whether it is a question of release of reserves, a request for an initial or an additional appropriation, or a request for additional legislative authority. We investigate each request for release of reserves as we would if it were a request for an additional appropriation. When the departmental representatives appear before the Bureau of the Budget to defend their annual requirements, we require them to show exactly how the funds made available for the year which just closed were spent, how the funds made available for the year in progress are being spent, and what they plan to do with the funds requested for the ensuing year. Through these various methods the Bureau exercises budgetary control, and the methods and procedures, including the incurrence of obligations by the departments, might be referred to as "Execution of the Budget."

Auditing.—As I have pointed out, the execution of the Budget concerns the legislative as well as the executive branch of the government. Congress is the fund-raising, fund-granting, and order-giving body, and it has the right and the duty of assuring itself that its orders have been faithfully executed. The chief continuing exercise of the power of Congress to control expenditures after the appropriation measures have been enacted is through the audit of public accounts by the General Accounting Office. Prior to 1921, this important function was lodged with the Treasury Department, under the immediate supervision of six auditors and the Comptroller of the Treasury, the latter's jurisdiction being confined principally to legal questions concerning appropriations and to passing upon appeals made by the departments from the auditors' decisions. The Budget and Accounting Act of 1921 abolished all of these offices and created in their place the General Accounting Office, headed by the Comptroller General. I shall not discuss here the functions of this important office, but shall limit myself to a consideration of the functions of the Bureau of the Budget.

Collateral functions of the Bureau.—In addition to the above-described work of the Bureau, it also exercises certain functions collateral to the preparation of the annual Budget. The most important of these collateral functions is that of advising the departments and agencies with respect to the relation of pending legislation or reports on pending legislation to the program of the President. The President has directed that there shall be submitted to the Bureau of the Budget, before submission to the Congress, or any committee or member thereof, each recommendation or report concerning proposed or pending legislation requested from or advanced by any executive department, independent establishment, or other government agency, or any officer thereof. The submitting agency will then be advised by the Bureau as to the relationship of the legislation, or of the report or recommendation thereon, to the program of the President; and when such recommendation or report is thereafter submitted to the Congress, or to a committee or member thereof, it must include a statement of the advice so received from the Budget Bureau.

Another function of the Bureau is to pass upon all enrolled bills that are received at the White House after their passage by the Congress. Before the President approves these bills, the Bureau of the Budget obtains the views and recommendations from the departments and agencies concerned, which are forwarded to the President with the Bureau's report and recommendation. If any of the reports and recommendations are unfavorable to the bill, the Bureau sees that a draft of veto message is sent along for the President's consideration.

The Bureau also passes upon, and in many cases prepares, all Executive Orders and Presidential Proclamations before they are submitted to the President, through the Department of Justice, for his approval.

There are other miscellaneous functions of the Bureau which I shall not go into here.

A great deal has been said about reorganization in Washington. The government has grown tremendously during the last six years, increasing the number of functions, adding new agencies, and has more than doubled the amount of its annual expenditures. The Budget Bureau, however, has tried to operate on about the same appropriation and with about the same number of employees it had in 1922. We decided last spring that it was high time for the Bureau to be reorganized and to secure additional personnel, in order not only to be better able to meet its increased responsibility under the enlarged governmental program, but to carry out to the fullest extent the intention of Congress as expressed in the Budget and Accounting Act of 1921.

In explaining the operations of the Bureau, I have elucidated the functions which the Bureau has performed during the past eighteen years. Some of these, it is true, have been more recently developed. But there is one section of the Budget and Accounting Act which has never been enforced, and yet to me it is one of the most important sections. I feel that if the Bureau had been properly equipped from the beginning to carry out this function, there would not be in Washington today any agitation, at least any need for agitation, for the reorganization of the governmental set up. The section referred to reads as follows:

> Sec. 209. The Bureau, when directed by the President, shall make a detailed study of the departments and establishments for the purpose of enabling the President to determine what changes (with a view of securing greater economy and efficiency in the conduct of the public service) should be made in (1) the existing organization, activities, and methods of business of such departments or establishments, (2) the appropriations therefor, (3) the assignment of particular activities to particular services, or (4) the regrouping of services. The results of such study shall be embodied in a report or reports to the President, who may transmit to Congress such report or reports or any part thereof with his recommendations on the matters covered thereby.

It is obvious that the authority contained in this section carries tremendous possibilities. But to proceed with the Bureau reorganization.

The new organization has been divided into four divisions, namely, Estimates, Fiscal, Coördination, and Investigation.

The Estimates Division will handle all estimates of appropriations. It will contain experts on every department and function of government. It will also work with the other divisions on any appropriation or legislative matter concerning the departments and agencies.

The Fiscal Division will prepare the Budget document, including all financial tables; estimate the expenditures under each item of appropriation; and prepare a draft of the Budget Message. It will also keep records of apportionments. In addition, I should like to see it continually study the Budget procedures of other countries, states and counties, with a view to improving our own budgetary procedure. It should strive to improve our financial statistics, so that the presentation to the public and to Congress can be clear and well-understood.

The Coördination Division will handle all problems which involve two or more departments, as well as all proposed legislation, reports on pending and proposed legislation, regulations requiring Presidential approval, and all Executive Orders and Proclamations.

The Investigation Division will be divided into two parts, viz., the Field Section and the Management Research Section. The Field Section will consist of a Washington office and eventually, I hope, four offices outside of Washington. There will be assigned to each field office definite territory, and it will be the duty of each office to know intimately every governmental activity and function within its territory, and whether there is any overlapping or duplication in such function, and if so, what steps should be taken to eliminate it. The offices will constantly be sending to the Bureau in Washington reports of these activities and functions in the field, so that the staff in the Bureau can have complete information about the whole government organization. The Management Research Section will continually study the whole government service with a view to increasing its efficiency of operation, eliminating overlapping, duplication, and superannuated offices. This is the division which will undertake specifically to carry out the provisions of Section 209 of the Budget and Accounting Act, to which I previously referred.

This whole organization must be made so flexible that the personnel from one division can be detailed to another division without any lost motion in training for the division to which the individuals are detailed. In other words, every employee must be trained to work in every division of the Bureau.

In conclusion I may say that I have great hopes for this revitalized Bureau of the Budget.

E. A. Goldenweiser

The Federal Reserve System Today

I PROPOSE to discuss briefly the Federal Reserve System as it exists and to bring out the contrast between the conception of the Federal Reserve System as we see it today and the ideas that were in the minds of those who established and organized it a quarter of a century ago. Since that time the entire outlook has changed fundamentally, reflecting great changes in the economic mechanism of the world. There are four different phases in the conception of the functions of the Federal Reserve System: (1) the banking function, (2) the monetary function, (3) the economic function, and (4) the political implications of the changes which have occurred.

The original conception of the Federal Reserve System was primarily that of a coöperative enterprise among member banks to pool their reserves, thus reducing the amount of reserves each would be obliged to hold individually and helping one another out by means of that pool, in case of extra strains caused by seasonal or cyclical changes. Business paper could be taken and rediscounted at the Federal Reserve Bank, and thus money would be made available for the granting of additional loans. There was also a great deal of stress laid upon the currency aspect of the new system, for the Federal Reserve System was the outcome of the stringency which arose periodically with respect to currency —the last crisis of this sort having occurred in 1907.

The original conception of the functions of the Federal Reserve System envisioned dollar-for-dollar contributions by the reserve banks in meeting temporary shortages of currency or credit. Those who planned the system had had no occasion to think in terms of multiple expansion of credit, on the basis of reserves. There was no idea, in the minds of the proponents of the system, of bank reserves as a base on which the credit structure is pyramided. Customary reserve requirements in England were working in much the same way as our own, but attention had never been directed to this phase of the problem. At the present time we think of reserves of member banks not so much as a reservoir gathered up from individual banks and concentrated at the Federal Reserve Banks, but as something that the reserve banks create in amounts adequate to serve as the basis of the total credit needed to finance the nation's business. The conception of the system as a mechanism for meeting an overflow of the demand for credit has been displaced by the idea that it is the business of the system to contribute to an adequate and continuous flow of credit through the channels of production and distribution. Banks have borrowed from the Reserve Banks—and that is almost an obsolete phrase now—for the purpose of making up the deficiency of reserves occurring as the net result of a great variety of operations consummated during the day. The idea of a direct relationship between the particular commercial transaction out of which the discounted paper originally arose and the use to which the reserve credit obtained by the discount was put, has dropped out of the picture. With it has gone the conception of liquidity as the fundamental basis of banking soundness. We think now in terms of an adequate supply of money to meet the country's needs and of adequate reserves to support such a money supply. The Federal Reserve System does not create the money, but merely the basis for it, as well as a propitious environment for its creation on that base. The System can also create an environment that encourages the destruction of an excessive money supply. Decisions as to which of these courses of action to pursue constitute Federal Reserve policy. This indicates briefly the manner in which the ideas of the proponents of the Federal Reserve System have been modified by experience.

The Federal Reserve System is still concerned, even more than at its beginning, with the safety of deposits. But in considering the safety of deposits, the Federal Reserve System thinks of them in different terms than do those who have more direct supervisory responsibility. The latter regard them chiefly from the point of view of protecting individual depositors' money, while the Federal Reserve System thinks of the safety of deposits chiefly from the point of view of maintaining a continuous and adequate flow of money. After 1929 the flow of money through the drawing of checks on deposit accounts suddenly ceased to work smoothly. Not only were demand deposits reduced by about 40 percent, but a check ceased to be money in the sense of the unquestioning acceptance of it as a medium of payment. There was doubt about the solvency of the bank on which the check was drawn, as well as about the solvency of the drawer.

Because of the necessity of protecting our money flow, this country has come to a partial acceptance of deposit insurance, which was highly unorthodox and which many opposed on the ground that bad banking would be encouraged. These arguments still have a measure of validity, but other considerations are more important. Economic events made us realize that we must not permit anything to happen that would disrupt the money flow. The Federal Deposit Insurance Corporation accomplishes a considerable part of the task, and it was accepted largely because of the disastrous consequences that followed upon the interruption of the money flow. The fact that the eligibility of paper has been broadened and that there is no longer much interest in the collateral back of Federal Reserve notes follows from the fundamental difference between the modern conception of the objectives of Federal Reserve policy, centering around an adequate and unobstructed flow of money, and the old conception which did not concern itself with such matters, but thought of the System simply as a source of supplementary funds to be used in emergencies. This change in viewpoint represents a transition from the strict banking conception of the System to the monetary conception.

When the System was organized, only rudimentary approaches to the monetary function were visualized. Open-market operations were to be engaged in, to supply the Federal Reserve System with funds "to make the discount rate effective." After the war, the course of events brought open-market operations into the foreground. Because of the factor of multiple expansion on the basis of reserves, the conception of open-market operations changed entirely. When the Reserve Banks bought securities in 1922 in order to build up their earnings, they found that discounts went down and earnings failed to increase. This taught the System a valuable lesson. It led to a formulation of the purposes of open-market operations. Open-market powers of the System were by resolution placed on the same basis as discount rates, by decreeing that they must be pursued with the view to accommodating commerce and business. This conception was later recognized in law. There are many who think the phrase is vague and dangerously elastic. But I like it because it is not rigid. We can read our own conceptions into it, and these conceptions may change with the times. The phrase saves us from incorporating past errors of judgment in immovable form, like so many public buildings which stand as monuments in stone to the bad taste or the misunderstandings of the past.

A great many new problems have come up in recent years because of the convulsions through which the world has gone. The silver policy and an enormous increase in reserves caused by the gold inflow are two of these. With excess reserves of about $3,-500,000,000, after reserve requirements had been increased by about $2,250,000,000, there is little room for open-market policies predicated on their influence on the volume of reserves. We have, in recent years, been talking about gold sterilization and other unheard of things, which could not have been in the minds of those who originally conceived the Federal Reserve System. They have been forced on us by post-war developments. The Federal Reserve System was thought out, planned, and organized when the whole world was on the gold standard. It is important to keep this fact in mind when considering the changes that have developed in the System since its inauguration. Much that is now thought of as due to different policies was caused by changes in international financial relationships. We are in an Alice in Wonderland of finance, because funds do not move from one country to another as the result of higher interest rates nor to correct trade balances; these influences have been subordinated to political developments and to changes in confidence in different currencies. We have gained in recent years $7,000,000,000 in gold, which represents primarily refugee money from Europe. The only time we have had any outflow was during a short period of doubt about the safety of funds in this country. This movement of money in and out of countries on a new basis, which has often looked like a flow uphill, is contrary to the fundamental basis of the old financial system, which had been built on the conception of funds moving in response to competitive price and rate relationships.

The broader economic functions of the Federal Reserve System—those not strictly monetary, or non-banking—are just beginning to be recognized. It is coming to be understood here and abroad that a monetary system cannot function in a vacuum. Such a system is circumscribed by the flow of money through various channels. It is related to methods of taxation. In taxation likewise the approach is gradually changing. It is no longer concerned exclusively with the problem of finding the least painful and most equitable way of raising needed funds. Tax authorities, as well as monetary authorities, should concern themselves with the maintenance of an unobstructed flow of money. The controversy over the tax on undistributed earnings dealt with the question of whether or not the tax would contribute to an even flow of income. This approach to the problem of taxation brings it closer to the monetary point of view. Similarly, problems of labor, of social security, of government spending, have a relationship to the money flow. A clearer understanding of these interrelationships is developing. Students of the subject usually understand these things fifty years before governments recognize them, and not infrequently cease to recognize them when the governments arrive at the point of doing so. One might almost say that this is the function of economic theorists—to pull in the opposite direction from current official trend.

This leads to my last point, namely, the political implications involved. We have a tradition of the desirability of the complete independence of the central bank from the government. In meetings of various economic groups after the war, during which the governments borrowed from the central banks and created disastrous inflation in Europe, the cry was raised that the central banks must be independent of the governments. This was even written into central-bank statutes. I should like here to define my conception of the independence of a central bank.

If by the independence of a central bank we mean that the central banks should pursue a policy in accordance with their own understanding, irrespective of governmental policy, then I say that independence is not only impossible but that it would be disastrous. What would happen in such a situation would be either that the central bank would be reorganized or that it would be sheared of its functions, which other institutions would be created to perform. To a certain extent this is what happened in this country. In 1933 the Federal Reserve System was not in sympathy with much that was being done by the government and opposed many of its measures. The consequence was that a whole series of institutions was established, with functions that could have been Federal Reserve functions and should have been closely coördinated with the Federal Reserve System. One difficulty was that the Federal Reserve System in 1933 was largely guided by the conceptions of 1913. A central bank must not remain on its Olympian heights.

I think of the independence of a central bank in terms of the understanding of monetary problems and of courage in pressing its point of view, in terms of a tradition commanding respect by the government and the public, and yet with recognition of the fact that it exercises governmental powers and must be a branch of the government.

In order to function in a democracy, it is essential, in entrusting powers to a government agency, to assume that they will be used for the public good, because adequate power to serve a public purpose inevitably involves its corollary, the power to do harm. If an agency is made completely safe, it is also made completely futile. Democracy is primarily a system that makes it possible to bring about change by other means than revolution. Public functions must be performed in the interest of the public good. Otherwise, the functionaries and the agencies themselves must be changed. Our fiscal problems and our monetary problems do not always call for the same solutions. This must be recognized and appreciated. If the central bank understands that it is its function to present the monetary point of view on current problems, and if it has succeeded in obtaining fair consideration of that point of view, then I think it has achieved all the independence that it should have.

We have always spoken of the Bank of England as being privately managed, privately owned, and as having no connection with the government. That is untrue, because the Issue Department is entirely in government hands, the amount of fiduciary issue being determined by the government. The Bank also works in close coöperation with the government in other matters. The Bank of England in its characteristic way preserves the appearance of complete independence, and at the same time realistically works out a program and gives advice which is taken into consideration. At the same time, the Bank does not act independently of the Treasury, nor the Treasury of the Bank. To quote from Governor Norman: "In monetary as in other matters the government of the day must have the final word."

Michael A. Heilperin

Fixed Parities and Fluctuating Exchanges as Objectives of Monetary Policy

AN INTERNATIONAL stabilization of currencies is not one of the problems which are in the foreground of current economic discussion. This results from two causes: in the first place, because political conditions are not ripe for any such manifestation of international coöperation; and, in the second place, because the prevailing fashion among economists favors the idea that to link national currencies to one another by bonds of fixed parities is not only undesirable but harmful.

If, in spite of this, the present subject has been chosen for discussion, it is because underneath the current glorification of monetary nationalism one can find a desire for stability. As Professor John H. Williams so rightly observes: [1]

> After cutting loose from the gold standard, what every country has done—save for the exchange control countries, where it seems obvious that some further action will be necessary—has been, in one degree or another and in one way or another, to tie back on again. . . . There is no evidence of any desire for a really flexible currency.

A mere declaration by the President of the United States or by the British Chancellor of the Exchequer to the effect that stabilization is desirable would suffice to bring the whole problem

[1] John H. Williams, "International Monetary Organization," *Lessons of Monetary Experience. Essays in Honor of Irving Fisher* (New York, 1937), pp. 33–34.

back into the limelight from which it has temporarily disappeared. A further reason for investigating these problems nowadays is precisely the remoteness, or apparent remoteness, of any constructive policy. During such periods it becomes the duty of economists, having then the leisure, to inquire into the mechanics of the solution of those problems which remain unsolved. It is in this spirit that the question of monetary stabilization will be discussed in the pages that follow.

THE PROBLEM OF MONETARY STABILITY

The question which must be dealt with at the very outset of our analysis is the following: Is monetary stability on an international scale a monetary problem in the technically narrow sense of the word, or is it, broadly speaking, an economic problem directly bearing upon the economic policies which relate to international trade and finance? Is it a problem susceptible of a monetary solution, or does its resolution imply the adoption of more complex measures, such as a revision of tariff policies, of regulations of foreign lending, and so forth?

Before answering this, let us define what is meant by international monetary stability. The term describes that situation in which the monetary units of the various countries bear a determined relationship one to another and in which this relationship remains steady in time. This, in turn, implies that balances of payments of the different countries remain in a state of durable equilibrium. Such equilibrium can result, however, only through the adoption of certain policies which will make it possible for corrective forces to be set in motion each time the balance of payments of a country shows a change—either surplus or deficit. Those corrective forces and the policies which release them are usually described as mechanisms of readjustment of balances of payments. Under the traditional gold standard, such mechanisms work through the dual instrumentality of changes in internal monetary circulations and the effects of such changes upon the internal prices of the various countries, on the one hand, and through differential changes in rates of interest on the other hand. I have attempted to show elsewhere, at greater length, that these two instrumentalities are the only ones susceptible of maintaining a long-run equilibrium in international payments.[2]

To put it briefly, a disturbance of equilibrium can be remedied either through changes taking place in the balance of trade of the countries in question, or through changes in the stream of financial operations. Provided there is no major cause of disturbance, momentary deficits or surpluses of balances of payments result principally from the uneven distribution in time of receipts and expenditures taking place across political boundaries. On account of this, a country may, at a certain time, receive many more payments from abroad than it has to make abroad, while later the reverse may be true. Short-term credit operations, which take place in response to differential shifts in rates of interest, will bridge over such maladjustments and smooth the course of international settlements.

Thus far there appears no need for the compensatory transactions to involve shifts in internal prices. It is very doubtful whether such shifts took place, to any appreciable extent, during the pre-war period of the functioning of the gold standard. While sufficient statistical information is unfortunately still lacking, it appears a likely hypothesis that the pre-war gold standard functioned, in the main, through the operation of the rate of interest and short-term credit transactions. There were, of course, certain general implications regarding price movements, about which a word will be said later, but it is unlikely that important changes in internal prices were associated with the working of the gold standard.

The situation becomes more intricate when balances of pay-

[2] M. A. Heilperin, *International Monetary Economics* (London and New York, 1939), Chapter VIII.

ments are subjected to major disturbances. Such disturbances may result from outside forces which are beyond human control, such as natural cataclysms of various sorts. They may be a consequence of changes in technique and in taste, which have repercussions upon the structure of international trade. Furthermore, they may result from political disturbances, either internal or international. And, finally, they may be due to systematic divergencies between the national economic and monetary policies pursued by various governments. This last point calls for further comment.

One of the assumptions implicitly underlying not only the traditional gold standard, but also any system of monetary internationalism, consists in the similarity of policies pursued in the different countries during the business cycle. While stable monetary conditions in the world help to bring about international coördination of cyclical movements and to produce an international spread of cyclical fluctuations, the adoption in the various phases of the cycle of similar policies is an important condition of the maintenance of that monetary stability.

There are a number of reasons for this interrelationship. The following two seem to be of outstanding importance:

In the first place, the fact that various countries find themselves at one and the same time in different stages of the business cycle, so that certain of them are depressed while others are prosperous, affects to a considerable extent capital movements. Not only will short-term credit transactions fail to take place in a way requisite to the functioning of the mechanisms of adjustment, but long-term investments will be made in favor of the prosperous countries and not of the depressed ones, with the further consequence that the former will tend to become more prosperous and the latter more depressed. We may infer, therefore, that the lack of synchronization of the cyclical movements will tend to increase the amplitude of such movements in all countries concerned. It is clear that under the strain of such conditions, unless controlled, monetary stability would break down sooner or later.

In the second place, the adoption of different types of business-cycle policy by countries which are at a given time in the same phase of the cycle will lead to important and systematic divergencies in the price developments taking place in each of the countries involved. This will affect the foreign trade of those countries and therefore their balances of payments, and it will be found that the effect will be both enduring and cumulative.

Since, in the absence of an internationally coördinated business-cycle policy, both types of consequences will follow, it is clear that there is an inescapable choice between national autonomy in economic policies and international monetary stability. Thus the problem of monetary stabilization is obviously much more than a question of one form or another of technical monetary organization. It involves the deeper-lying issue between economic nationalism, on the one hand, and economic internationalism on the other.

Frequently, when discussing international stabilization, one refers to the notion of monetary parities. It is interesting to note that this term, which appears so often in economic literature, is very rarely properly defined. The definition proposed here envisages monetary parity as being that rate of exchange between two currencies which can be maintained over long periods of time without exercising any strain either on the internal economic life of the country concerned or on the state of international economic relations.

When, in the midst of a period of international currency disturbances, we discuss the future of monetary stability, obviously we are confronted with the task of postulating, at some time in the future, new parities between currencies (provided, of course, that one favors stabilization as the goal of future policies). In this case, is it possible to say beforehand, and on the basis of the available economic data, what the appropriate relation between any two currencies will be? The prevalent view seems to be that such an a priori determination of parities is possible, at least with a certain degree of precision. The school of thought which holds this view most consistently adheres to the conception of what Professor Cassel has called "purchasing power parities." The notion is too familiar to require detailed discussion here. Briefly, the theory is based on the idea that changes in parities are entirely due to changes in national price levels. It infers from that postulate a method of calculating a new parity, after a period of monetary disturbances. The procedure is very simple. One applies to the old parity the quotient of changes in price levels taking place during the period envisaged, and thus one obtains the new parity. There are numerous economists who consider this merely a general indication of the order of magnitude of the new parity, and who allow for a certain elasticity in determining the new relation. But the general idea is that, starting with the available data, one can figure out an approximately correct relationship between currencies.

Personally, I am inclined to doubt whether such a position is acceptable. It would be valid, in a world in which there existed no financial transactions whatever and in which international trade was uniquely determined by differential changes in price levels. But such is not the world in which we happen to live. In our universe financial transactions play an extremely important part, and international trade depends on many other elements than changes in the statistical construction known as the price level. The influence of financial transactions seems to be all too often disregarded or to be emphasized inadequately. If a rate chosen as parity is not one in the enduring character of which financial circles in the various countries have full confidence, credit operations of different types will result, not excluding flights of capital, and this may suffice completely to upset the stability of such rate, even in the absence of any further price movements.

It is very instructive, from this point of view, to investigate the French monetary developments between 1937 and 1939. Even if it should appear to be less satisfactory, from an intellectual point of view, than a priori parities, the notion of a posteriori parities must, I think, be given preference over the former. It is always better to deal with a concept which is clumsy, but adequate, than with one which is inadequate, though elegant.

HAS THE GOLD STANDARD BEEN A FAILURE?

The familiar phrase that nothing succeeds like success applies to monetary systems as it does to human individuals. We might add that nothing seems to fail so much as lack of success. This may explain the discredit into which the gold standard has fallen in many circles since 1930. It is true that advocates of that system can point to the great expansion of international trade and of national prosperity during the fifty years prior to the World War, during which the gold standard became a generalized monetary system. It is also true that they can point to the distress that accompanied the breakdown of international monetary stability. But critics of the gold standard can answer that the depression was deepest before the breakdown of international monetary stability, that the gold standard did nothing to prevent the depression, that after 1931 the sterling area, which was off the gold standard, fared economically very much better than the gold-bloc countries, and that improvement in economic conditions in France followed the surrender of the gold standard.

But do such appeals to historic facts decide the issue in favor of or against gold? It seems clear that they do not. All of them exemplify the dangerous logical procedure called *argumentum post hoc propter hoc*. There were many reasons for the expansion of international trade and of prosperity in the pre-war days. It was the growth of economic internationalism which rendered possible the extension of monetary internationalism, which in turn became a factor favoring greater international coöperation. It is equally true that a system of monetary internationalism could not survive an almost complete collapse of international coöperation in other spheres of economic life. If the gold standard broke down, it was on account of the conditions under which it had to work. It was not within the powers of the system to affect those conditions. The gold standard was neither the cause of prosperity nor the cause of distress. It was simply and solely a monetary system that could work only under certain conditions, which failed to be satisfied long before the ultimate collapse of the system.

The modern criticism of international monetary stability (and of the gold standard) seems to be very much influenced by historic experiences, some of which have already been cited. Let us look carefully into one or two of these experiences.

England after 1925.—It is true that after the return to gold, England entered upon a period of economic difficulties from which the country did not emerge until after 1931. To be sure, this has been attributed more often to the parity at which gold payments were resumed in 1925 than to the fact of returning to gold. But the implication remained that England was more prosperous after going off the gold standard than during the six years of adherence to the system. While essentially in agreement with the thesis according to which England mistakenly returned to a parity that was too high, and therefore had to undergo a process of deflation which was both painful and difficult to carry out, I should nevertheless like to point to certain more fundamental factors, which may explain England's difficulties in the late twenties.

In the first place, there was a growing trend toward economic nationalism, which found expression in the difficulties of England's export trade. Certain industries were affected by technological changes abroad. Consequently, there was much need for internal industrial adjustments, which at that time failed to be realized. André Siegfried's *England's Crisis* [3] will be found of interest, in this connection. No amount of monetary manipulation could have helped England out of difficulties due to such important structural factors. The period after 1931 was not only one of monetary changes, but also one of considerable reorganization in certain British industries, and it will be noted that the so-called spatial areas continue to exist, in spite of the depreciation of sterling, in spite of the young British protectionism, and in spite, even, of the development of war economy.

France's experiences after 1931 supply another favorite argument for those who object to the gold standard. However, the situation of France and the gold bloc is rather peculiar. The gold bloc was formed, it will be remembered, at the London Conference of 1933, and during its short life it was nothing more than a designation covering a group of five countries which persisted in keeping the pre-depression price of gold, while the world price of gold was changed by between 40 and 50 percent. This way of putting it is perhaps not quite correct, but the circumstances referred to are as follows.

After 1931, the countries of the so-called sterling area devalued their currencies by about 40 percent. In 1933 the United States devalued the dollar by 49 percent. From December, 1933, until the fall of 1938, the relation between the dollar and sterling was almost stable. We may therefore speak of a change in the price of gold taking place *de facto* over the greater part of the world. Under these conditions, it was France, Belgium, Holland, Switzerland, and Poland which carried out what I have described before as an autonomous economic policy. For once, the adherence to gold was an expression of non-coöperation rather than of co-

[3] London, 1931.

operation, a paradoxical situation, to be sure, but one the particular characteristics of which should be clearly recognized. It was only after the collapse of the gold bloc that a chance for rebuilding monetary internationalism reappeared. For the time being, of course, nothing was done in this direction. We must emphasize once more the fact that while France was on the gold standard, this was in no correct sense an international gold standard, because at that time there happened to be no such thing in existence.

It follows from the foregoing observations that the facts of recovery in countries off the gold standard and of a continued depression in countries on the gold standard in the years 1933–36 are not proof of the adequacy or nonadequacy of an international gold standard as a monetary system. They do demonstrate, however, the advantages of international coöperation and of the stability of exchanges. It will be noted that during the period 1931–33 exchange rates were fairly stable within the sterling area, and that after the end of 1933 stability existed within the sterling-dollar area. It is also apparent that under these circumstances there was a notable improvement in trade among countries belonging to this area. In this sense, one can speak of a gradual revival of a *de facto* monetary internationalism within a limited group of countries.

THE IMPORTANCE OF INTERNATIONAL ECONOMIC COÖPERATION

All our foregoing observations tend to the same conclusion: international coöperation is an essential condition of monetary stability. In the light of this conclusion, it will be interesting to analyze the post-war monetary reconstruction. It will be found that this reconstruction was not based on any comprehensive degree of economic coöperation. While the international conferences of Brussels (1920) and of Genoa (1922) emphasized the importance of such coöperation, and while the latter of these conferences suggested that a meeting of central banks be called to discuss the common problem of monetary reconstruction, nothing has been done in that direction.[4] Events thus led to the adoption of a monetary system which was developed amidst a growing trend toward economic nationalism. Like a skyscraper built on quicksands, the construction collapsed under the impact of the first storm. It is interesting to note that not even the founding of the Bank for International Settlements was preceded by a conference of central banks, nor by the elaboration of an international monetary convention. The bank, it is true, was the outcome of a desire for monetary internationalism and of an attempt to solve the reparations problem. And it is also true that the latter attempt died out, prematurely and unregretted.

In effect, therefore, a center of international monetary coöperation was established in the first year of the depression. But it was given very inadequate powers to achieve wider objectives and it was forced to work under extremely unfavorable conditions. It is an institution, therefore, which still has to prove itself and which will be unable to do so until there is a revival of economic coöperation in the widest sense of the word.

The first post-war decade was pervaded by an atmosphere of compromise, and nowhere was the compromise more evident and less regarded than in the contrast between the growth of commercial nationalism, on the one hand, and the attempts at monetary reconstruction on the other. The gold exchange standard was, to a certain extent, the outcome of this compromise.

While it would lie beyond the scope of the present discussion to consider in detail the causes of the monetary breakdown, we may say that its occurrence marked the victory of nationalism over internationalism, in the post-war world. We are still living under the consequences of this victory.

[4] William E. Rappard, "Post-War Efforts for Freer Trade," *Geneva Studies,* Vol. IX, No. 2, Geneva, Geneva Research Centre, 1938.

OBJECTIVES OF POLICY

What are the conclusions which may be drawn from the foregoing discussion, as regards the outlook for the future?

As indicated in our title, the alternatives, in terms of monetary technique, are a return to fixed parities, on the one hand, and the maintenance of a system of fluctuating exchanges on the other. The ultimate answer will depend on the solution found for the broader issue of nationalism versus international coöperation. At the present time, there is a considerable section of professional opinion which favors so-called flexible exchanges. What does this suggestion imply?

Flexible exchanges are apparently such movements of exchange rates as would correspond to changes in the relative price levels in the various countries. More precisely, on the assumption that the various countries have divergent price movements, flexible exchanges will bring about the needed adjustment among the national currencies. The system, therefore, is intended to combine a considerable degree of national autonomy with a not-inconsiderable degree of stability in international trade. In the words of one of the leading advocates of flexible exchanges, the following state of affairs can be achieved: "If, instead of absolute stability of exchange rates, an attempt were made to adjust rates proportionately to shifts in the relative domestic purchasing powers of the several currencies it would be possible for any nation to pursue whatever internal monetary policy it judged appropriate to its interest without significant disturbance of international commercial and financial relations." [5]

It is hoped, therefore, to reconcile the apparently hostile objectives of nationalism and internationalism. Personally, I confess I cannot entertain such hopes. National monetary and economic autonomy leads to the adoption of more and more nationalistic

[5] Frank D. Graham, *Journal of the American Statistical Association,* Vol. XXXIII, No. 204, p. 773.

measures, as the experience of the last ten years clearly shows. I have already mentioned some of the consequences of nationally independent business-cycle developments. Let us add that, under such conditions, a resumption of long-term investment abroad is neither likely nor advisable, while short-term credit transactions are likely to continue to be large and erratic. If this is so—and there seems to be much to confirm this view and little to contradict it—then exchanges which are not stable will be subjected, under certain conditions, to fluctuations, the scope of which will render inadequate the use of the term flexible—they will be chaotically unstable. Were it not for the desire for stability, we would have seen, within the last few years, much wider fluctuations of exchange rates than those actually experienced.

As Professor Williams remarks:

> The United States, after going off gold definitively in April, 1933, had returned to a fixed buying and selling price of gold by the end of January, 1934. England, which is commonly cited as the country least willing or likely to return to the gold standard, has been acting essentially like a managed gold standard country virtually from the day she went off gold. The Equalization Account, as thus far operated, has been a device, not merely for ironing out day-to-day fluctuations, but for preventing a rise, and perhaps at times a fall, in the pound, by means of an international gold flow to and from England. Had England really wanted a flexible currency she would have allowed the pound to rise against the franc as capital took flight to London, which might have prevented the second devaluation of the franc. But no one would have seriously advised such a course. The rise in terms of the franc would have been a rise also in terms of other currencies, including the dollar, which would have recreated England's problem, and would in any case have led to a subsequent fall when the capital flowed out again. England has, therefore, though officially off gold, accumulated more gold than ever before in her history.[6]

That the system of flexible exchanges has worked so well recently, is because ultimate stability, as an objective of policy, has

[6] Williams, *op. cit.*, pp. 33–34.

never been entirely lost sight of. There is no doubt that this system provides a workable expedient in peculiarly unstable times. Nobody could be more emphatic than I in warning against too early a return to monetary internationalism, in the midst of a nationalistic world. But one must not confuse an expedient with a solution. To make the best of a bad job must not be mistaken for doing a good job, and we are very far indeed from doing a good job in the field of international economic relations.

Similarly, exchange equalization or stabilization funds cannot be viewed as a radically new departure in the field of monetary organization. They are very useful, indeed, in helping to maintain a maximum of exchange stability amidst unfavorable conditions. They will remain very useful as long as major disturbances in international flows of capital take place without being apparent. Their further existence may, indeed, make the future system of monetary internationalism safer and more stable. But there is nothing in these funds that exceeds the possible scope of operations of a central bank. Given adequate financial possibilities, any central bank could do what exchange funds are doing at the present time.

If exchange funds can and, as I think, should, be integrated into the monetary system of the future, exchange control must of course be abolished. By exchange control I mean the concentration in the hands of a public authority of *all* the dealings in foreign exchanges. It can be shown, though I refrain from doing so here,[7] that exchange control, thus defined, leads progressively to the establishment of a more or less comprehensive control by the state over the economic activity of the country. The continued existence of exchange control stands in direct opposition to the continued existence of democratic political institutions. It is a system of monetary organization that can exist only under a regime of totalitarian state socialism. Since, in envisaging the

[7] Heilperin, *op. cit.*, pp. 237–45.

future organization of the world, one cannot discuss monetary problems in a political vacuum, but must take into account both monetary and non-monetary elements of social life, exchange control must be ruled out by whoever favors democratic and liberal institutions. This may mean, of course, that a revived economic internationalism will be limited to a certain group of countries only. However that be, I wish to emphasize again how very dangerous too much compromise can be.

Fixed parities appear to me to be the objective of that monetary policy which best comports with a revival of economic internationalism and with the maintenance of liberalism. If events should carry us in this direction, it is probable that the reëstablishment of fixed parities would be accomplished gradually and progressively. The Bank for International Settlements, with properly revised statutes, would be a very helpful instrument of action, both in administering monetary coöperation among large financial centers and in helping the spread of monetary stability throughout the world. In order to fulfill that function, the Bank should receive, in the form of a monetary convention, the basis it lacks for its operation; while participating membership might have to be restricted to countries which do not practice exchange control.

L. R. Rounds

Industrial Loans
And Federal Reserve Banks

THE ASSIGNMENT given me is to tell you something of the operations of the Federal Reserve banks in the industrial loan field.

As you probably know, these operations, so far as reserve banks are concerned, really resulted from criticisms of the commercial banks for their unwillingness to make loans to borrowers. Such criticisms were very frequent during the early days of the depression, and finally led to legislation designed to broaden the powers of the Federal Reserve System in making loans. The first such step was taken in the summer of 1933 with an amendment to the Federal Reserve Act authorizing the Reserve Banks to make loans to individuals and corporations on eligible paper. That particular amendment did not liberalize the lending powers of the banks except as to whom a loan could be made. Very few loans were made under this amendment because it quickly developed that the situation could not be met by confining requirements to eligible paper, that is, paper issued in settlement of a commercial transaction, paper which, in theory at least, would be self-liquidating, the loan being repaid within ninety days at the most. Loans confined to that type of paper did not meet the situation which existed in the early days of the depression. The demand was for long-term, not short-term credit.

A year later, in June, 1934, the Reserve Act was further

amended by the addition of Section 13b. This had the effect of removing most of the restrictions as to the type of paper and its self-liquidating character. The reserve banks were authorized to make loans to established concerns for working capital purposes ("working capital" in the sense of funds which are used in the current operations of the business,—for example, in a manufacturing business, to produce inventory, to carry accounts receivable, etc., not capital to be used for building a plant), and only in cases where the loans could not be readily obtained elsewhere on reasonable terms. Such loans could not be made for a period longer than five years. Loans could not be made to finance a new industry. The policy throughout has been to be liberal in the interpretation of these terms and to try to make loans wherever there was a reasonable basis for so doing and to avoid technicalities as much as possible. In some cases borrowers have been permitted to use a part of the loan for additions or improvements to plant, if such use of the funds appeared to be necessary and if the condition of the borrower justified it. But on the whole, loans have of course been largely restricted to providing working capital.

When operations began the bank was besieged with applications. In the summer of 1934 and for a year after, a large number of inquiries were received, altogether about 5,000. Some 1,500 of these resulted in actual applications which were made with the submission of full data regarding the business enterprise. The difference between the 5,000 and 1,500 was largely made up of cases which were ineligible for loans—financing real estate, personal loans, etc.; that is, they were not for "working capital" and, therefore, could not be granted; and of course a good many were hopeless, quite obviously so, after even brief study. Applications were encouraged in all cases where there appeared any likelihood at all that a loan could be made. Out of the 1,500 applications received, about 500 were actually approved, or roughly one-third, for an aggregate amount of some $30,000,000. There were actually put on the books some 358 loans for an aggregate amount of about $26,000,000. Of these, 263 have been repaid in full; 83 have had some payments made; while 12 have had no payments made. About half of these loans were made directly to the borrowing institution or business, and the other half were made by a commercial bank with an arrangement under which the Reserve Bank shared the risk. Under this arrangement, the commercial bank actually making the loan must assume at least 20 percent of the risk, the Reserve Bank taking not more than 80 percent. Quite a number of banks here in New York did a considerable amount of business on this basis. In all such cases the Reserve Bank gave the lending institution a written commitment or agreement with respect to the division of the risk, and also agreed at any time upon demand to purchase the entire loan, thus assuring the lending institution of liquidity at all times with respect to such loans. Very few of these loans were ever sold to the Reserve Bank. In practically all cases they were carried by the lending institution throughout the entire period of the loan.

In the early days of this operation we found some instances where commercial banks appeared to have been over-conservative in their lending policies. However, there is much to be said on the other side. Applicants were for the most part small business men who had only one bank account, and frequently that bank had closed or been merged with another institution. Many such applicants were not sufficiently well known to their new bank of account to secure a line of credit. It takes time to do that. A bank feels it wants to know something about a business before it considers extending credit, a very natural precaution. When we consider the conditions that existed at that time, it is perhaps not surprising that credit was not easy to get. There has been a marked change in this situation during the past two or three years. This is evidenced strongly by the falling off in applications for industrial loans. At this particular moment there is not a single application on file in the Federal Reserve Bank of New York, and a new application has not been received within the past two months.

The large amount of excess reserves, and the problem of the banks to secure sufficient income to pay expenses, has been a powerful factor affecting loaning policy. Banks today, by and large, are about as free with credit as banks ever should be. Of course, allowances must be made for the fact that there are always differences of opinion about particular businesses and a particular loan application. One bank might refuse an application for a loan and another might make it. This matter of providing credit is not a simple one. Some people appear to think if a man is in business there ought to be some place he can go and get credit, take it away, use it, and bring it back. But anyone who is actually operating in the business of lending money, especially other people's money, realizes that there is a great deal more to it than that.

The problems of business are complex. One can take an application for a loan, study the history of the business and its financial situation, feel it to be a business that has prospects, and perhaps make a loan, only to find three months later that everything that he thought about that situation was wrong. While we are on that point, let me tell you about one loan that we made. This particular loan, in justice to our organization, was made against our better judgment, as far as the general credit picture was concerned. It was a loan that was sorely needed by the community. We had no confidence in the long-term outcome of that particular business, but we did think that with competent management it could in the particular circumstances which existed operate for one year, manufacture its product and turn it into cash and pay back the loan, even though the business as a whole was not ultimately successful. The maximum loss possible appeared small.

Other conditions appeared to justify making the loan. Due to its location we relied on another institution to follow the situation. At the end of the year we found that this particular business, through incompetent management and other reasons, came to the end of the season with about half of the money borrowed invested in raw material inventory which could not be moved, for which there was no demand and very little chance of working it off. This is an illustration of what can happen. In this connection perhaps it should be stated that the reserve bank tries to be realistic about these loans. No loans are made which it is not believed can be collected. At the same time loans have been made which had a higher element of risk than any commercial bank should take. These risks were taken in view of prevailing conditions in an attempt to be helpful during this period and to test the whole general credit structure—to make what might be called perhaps a "noble experiment" in the field of industrial loans. Naturally a few have been made which cannot be collected.

Much study has been given in an attempt to determine if there is a real need for these loans. It has been frequently stated that credit is not available to many who need it. An effort has been made to secure information on this point. Following the Small Business Men's Conference held in Washington not quite a year ago, which got a great deal of publicity, an association was organized here in New York for the purpose of investigating the extent to which credit was not available to the small business man. This organization was known as the Smaller Business Association of New York, New Jersey and Connecticut. The association received encouragement from various sources. It organized a banking committee which sent out a large number of questionnaires to small business people designed to get information as to the need for credit; 6,000 replies were received, most of which evidenced a need for credit. This banking committee made a sincere effort to go through those applications and see what could be done about it. The letters were sorted into three piles, A, B and C. A included cases which perhaps had some merit. In B were those thought not to have merit, and in C those which appeared obviously without merit. The chairman of the committee appealed to the Clearing House for help and asked if some of the banks would not lend their credit men to assist the committee in reviewing these questionnaires or applications to determine which had merit, and if possible to assist in finding ways to get credit. Banks were quite coöperative. Then the committee asked us to provide space for the work which was the first we knew of the operation. It seemed like a mistake to ask bank men to make this investigation, since the banks were themselves under criticism, and it was suggested that the New York Credit Men's Association be asked to assist by assigning a committee of credit men from industries. Arrangements were made for a preliminary discussion to review a number of these applications to see what basis there was for a study.

When these applications were actually produced, it was apparent that they did not include sufficient information to enable any committee to determine whether or not credit would be justified in the particular case. These applications, which were in the nature of a questionnaire, outlined some principles and listed twelve questions on a single sheet of paper. Some of the questions were—

"What is the character of the business."

"Do you need capital, if so how much."

"What was the total volume of business done last year."

No provision was made for either a balance sheet or a profit and loss statement. The committee from the Smaller Business Association apparently had not realized the inadequacy of its information and was greatly disappointed that something could not be done with the 6,000 questionnaires or applications which it had received.

As a means of relieving the situation the reserve bank offered to review in detail the cases of 100 of those who had filed applications if the Smaller Business Association would select the cases and arrange for them to come to the bank. Subsequently the association selected 100 names, in each case writing a letter and later following it up with a telephone call suggesting that the applicant come to the Federal Reserve Bank. At the same time the bank also wrote a letter inviting them to come and discuss their problems, and telling them what information it would be helpful for them to bring in order that the bank might have an understanding of their problem. After some weeks there finally came in a total of 49 out of the 100. All of these cases were reviewed in detail. Six cases were found where the applicants appeared to be entitled to credit and to be in a position to give good security for it. As none of them had previously approached their own banks, it was suggested that they do so and if difficulty were experienced they were invited to return to the reserve bank. None of this group was later heard from. Eight other cases were found where it was felt there was sufficient merit to justify a more careful review, and each one in this group was encouraged to file a formal application for a loan. The remaining 35 appeared quite definitely not to justify a loan. Of the 8 who were encouraged to file applications just one actually filed, and this application after the usual investigation was approved for a loan, but the loan was not made as the applicant's bank of account agreed to make it instead.

Subsequently the committee of the Smaller Business Association sent out similar letters to some 200 names of those who had filed questionnaires or applications, inviting them to come to the Reserve Bank for an interview. The Reserve Bank did not write to this group as the experience with the first 100 names did not appear to justify it. However, between 30 and 40 of those written to by the association actually did visit the bank, but none of those who were interviewed appeared to justify a loan. On the basis of the record if we look only at the list of 6,000 small business concerns which filed a questionnaire indicating a need for loans, it might be thought that there was a serious need for credit in this field.

Of course, there will always be people who need credit and cannot get it, but, in the last analysis, the chap who is lending money, especially other people's money, must exercise final judgment. He cannot accept the judgment of the borrower in all cases. Furthermore, a great deal of the so-called need for credit is need for capital, equity capital. Undoubtedly, there has been some tightening up of the sources of equity capital during the depression years, and it has not been easy to get, but bank credit should not have to pick up the load previously carried by the investor.

It should also be kept in mind that most of the successful business corporations of today achieved their success by plowing back earnings into the business, and many of them were not in any stage of their existence large users of credit. It is well to have in mind, in the case of many of our very largest corporations, that the greater part of their present capital was neither invested nor borrowed but is represented by earnings retained in the business.

The law under which these operations have been conducted by the Reserve Banks provides for a review of all applications by a committee of five business men, which makes a recommendation to the bank. The bank is not required to follow these recommendations, but it must get them. This committee has done an excellent job. In general its views and those of the bank have not differed greatly.

I have here some financial statements of actual business concerns to which we have made loans (see the tables at the end of the chapter):

(A) This was a medium-sized concern in the machine tool industry representing a consolidation of a number of small companies. The consolidation had never been completely digested before the depression, when they were pretty hard hit. The head of this concern came to the bank in October of 1934. He stated that he did not want the money for some time but wanted to know where he could get it when he did need it. An application for $350,000 was approved, but the loan was not actually made until December, 1936. During that period the company was reorganized, bondholders becoming owners of the business, which is evidenced by a large increase in net worth. Progress began to be apparent, in 1935 the business showing a cash gain before depreciation, and in 1936 a net profit after depreciation. The business continued to show progress with increasing profits. The entire loan was repaid in 1938, and no borrowing has been done since. Note that the current ratio in 1934 when commitment was given was approximately even, while in 1938 there were nearly three dollars of current assets for one of liabilities. This business was evidently helped by a loan and is an illustration of what good management can do with a business.

(B) The applicant in this case was a paper manufacturer. While progress is not quite so spectacular as in the previous case, it is nevertheless steady and substantial. An application for $200,000 was approved, but only $125,000 was actually borrowed, as that was all that was needed. The loan has been entirely repaid. Note the improvement in current assets from less than two to one in 1934, to nearly five to one in 1937.

(C) The applicant in this case was an iron mine. The business was flat, overhead expenses were heavy; the purpose of the loan was to get the ore out and provide a means of living to the community. Three loans were made altogether, aggregating $600,000. Substantial progress has been made. Loan has since been repaid in full.

These three loans are looked upon as having been successful

operations. The borrower was helped and the bank got its money back. The next three were less satisfactory:

(D) The applicant was a manufacturer of pleasure yachts, power boats, and so forth. It should be noted that the figures in the years prior to the application, appearing in the first two or three columns, indicate a much better position than in the three previous illustrations. In this case a loan for $50,000 was made, followed by a second $50,000. The business appeared to do fairly well in 1936 and 1937, but in 1937 the inventory increased from $135,000 to $300,000, which was definitely a danger signal. Investigation showed that while the business had done a very large volume that year, it appeared to have been accomplished by liberal trade-in allowances so that the inventory consisted largely of second-hand boats, with the result that a large loss was taken the following year. Failure to know costs was an important factor in the lack of success in this business.

(E) The applicant was a small manufacturing stationer. Previous banks had not had a satisfactory experience. A loan of $25,000 was granted and has since been repaid. Nevertheless experience is looked upon as unsatisfactory as the business made no progress, net current assets showing a steady decline. Loan was not repaid from earnings.

(F) The applicant was a manufacturer of motor trucks. Business has continued to be unsuccessful and is now in process of liquidation. It is expected loan will be repaid in full although there may be a small loss.

A study was recently made of those loans which have been entirely repaid, with a view to determining how many of the borrowers had really benefited from the loans. For this purpose we attempted to divide these borrowers into three classes: First, those who had definitely benefited, and we found that 46 percent of them fell in this class; second, those who had derived no apparent benefit, and we found 23 percent fell in this class. The remainder, 31 percent, were borderline cases which could not definitely be said to have benefited, but these borrowers had at least held their own. In this connection it is necessary to have in mind the recession which overtook a lot of borrowers in the middle of this program. If there had been no second depression, a number of the loans which have given trouble would have come out all right.

One other study has been made. That was of the applications which have been declined, with a view to seeing how many showed a need for equity capital as contrasted with credit, and how many applications represented a fair prospect for the investment of equity capital, that is from the investors' point of view. Seven hundred and fifty-four declined applications were reviewed. Fifteen cases were found, aggregating about two million dollars, as representing what was considered to be a good prospect for the employment of capital. Sixty-nine applications, aggregating four million dollars, were considered as offering only fair prospects for the employment of equity capital. The remaining six hundred and seventy applications were considered as poor prospects for investment. This classification was based on all of the information we had about each of these businesses, which information in most cases went back for a period of ten years.

An officer of Dun & Bradstreet recently made a study of the rapidity of turnover of American business enterprises, the results of which have been published. During the period from 1915 to 1935 there were at all times approximately 2,000,000 business concerns in the United States. In each year during that period approximately 400,000 of these concerns, or 20 percent, went out of business, their places being taken by an equal number of new enterprises. This in itself speaks volumes on the hazards of extending credit to business enterprises, large or small.

CASE A

(In thousands)

	12/31/28	12/31/30	12/31/32	6/30/34	6/14/35 *	12/31/35	12/31/36	12/31/37	9/30/38
Cash	$ 50	$ 60	$ 36	$ 38	$ 167	$ 33	$ 37	$ 31	$ 49
Receivables	180	109	174	50	22	90	133	158	88
Inventory	1,038	705	593	536	281	301	348	601	759
Total cur. assets	1,268	874	803	624	470	424	518	790	896
Plant	4,977	3,015	2,657	4,385	3,165	3,170	3,151	3,188	1,442
Other assets	18	11	73	85	284	263	268	252	242
Total	$6,263	$3,900	$3,533	$5,094	$3,919	$3,857	$3,937	$4,230	$2,580
Due banks	50		184	90	51	20	(A) 68	(A) 125	(A) 165
" trade	176	40	15	5	46	48	63	144	116
Accruals	77	40	(A) 187	(A) 427	91	82	45	65	38
Misc. liab.	8	5	26	47	60	12	23	10	
Total cur. liab.	311	85	412	569	248	162	199	344	319
Deferred liab.					189	(A) 186	(A) 97	(A) 90	
Mtge. bonds	2,552	2,239	2,232	2,232					
Total debt	2,863	2,324	2,644	2,801	437	348	296	434	319
Res. for deprec.	†	†	†	1,864	1,402	1,470	1,586	1,661	†
Net worth	3,400	1,576	889	429	2,080	2,039	2,055	2,135	2,261
Total	$6,263	$3,900	$3,533	$5,094	$3,919	$3,857	$3,937	$4,230	$2,580
	12 Mos.	*12 Mos.*	*12 Mos.*	*12 Mos.*	*6½ Mos.*	*6½ Mos.*	*12 Mos.*	*12 Mos.*	*9 Mos.*
Cash gain	$ 267	$	$	$	$	$ 35	$ 150	$ 226	$ 232
Depreciation	187	164	93	47	51	75	140	139	107
Net income	80						10	87	125
			(A) $169M Interest	(A) $404M Interest		(A) $165M 13b loan	(A) 13b loan	(A) $75M 13b loan Current, $90M Deferred	(A) $90M 13b loan

* New company after reorganization.
† Plant is net of reserve for depreciation.

CASE B

(In thousands)

	12/31/28	*12/31/30*	*12/31/32*	*12/31/34* *	*12/31/35*	*12/31/36*	*12/31/37*
Cash	$ 81	$ 42	$ 49	$ 15	$ 59	$ 72	$ 157
Receivables	634	414	234	239	209	221	157
Inventory	868	740	439	339	292	302	269
Total cur. assets	1,583	1,196	722	593	560	595	583
Plant	1,643	1,624	1,647	1,670	1,690	1,682	1,695
Other assets	64	59	29	23	39	13	13
Total	$3,290	$2,879	$2,398	$2,286	$2,289	$2,290	$2,291
Due banks	100		121	110	(A) 39	(A) 47	(A) 27
Due trade	31	55	47	69	55	89	37
Accruals & res.	14	12	5	29	48	37	54
Other liabs.	173	158	48	137	1		
Total cur. liabs.	318	225	221	345	143	173	118
Def'd liabs.	187	187	221	100	(A) 308	(A) 261	234
Total debt	505	412	442	445	451	434	352
Res. for deprec.	478	539	608	694	743	768	817
Net worth	2,307	1,928	1,348	1,147	1,095	1,088	1,122
Total	$3,290	$2,879	$2.398	$2,286	$2,289	$2,290	$2,291

	12 Mos.	*12 Mos.*	*12 Mos.*	*12 Mos.*	*12 Mos.*	*12 Mos.*	*12 Mos.*
Cash gain	$ 110	$	$	$	$	$ 57	$ 83
Depreciation	44	44	42	46	48	51	49
Net income	66					6	34
					(A) 113M 13b loan $39M Current $74M Def.	(A) $74M 13b loan $47M Current $27M Def.	(A) 13b loan

* Last statement before 13b loan advanced.

CASE C

(In thousands)

	12/31/25	12/31/28	12/31/31	12/31/32	12/31/33	12/31/34 *	12/31/35	12/31/36	12/31/37
Cash	$ 42	$ 185	$ 44	$ 69	$ 35	$ 22	$ 138	$ 376	$ 384
Receivables	192	607	158	211	141	119	167	330	124
Inventory	954	821	1,237	817	610	432	426	284	656
Total cur. assets	1,188	1,613	1,439	1,097	786	573	731	990	1,164
Plant	17,919	17,157	16,610	16,601	16,151	16,068	15,982	15,776	15,562
Invest. & adv. to affil.	513	378	466	477	840	695	933	935	874
Other assets	572	532	579	587	77	66	86	84	90
Total	$20,192	$19,680	$19,094	$18,762	$17,854	$17,402	$17,732	$17,785	$17,690
Due banks / Due trade	{ 1,647	{ 253	{ 668	{ 834					
Due banks					150	150	(A)121	(A) 99	93
Due trade					379	180	67	125	76
Accruals	372	544	304	603			225	240	233
Other liabs.							227	227	227
Total cur. liabs.	2,019	797	972	1,437	529	330	640	691	629
Deferred liabs.	173	2,172	2,169	2,169			(B)230	(B)290	(B)210
Mtge. bonds	3,600	3,600	3,600	3,600	3,578	3,562	3,553	3,551	3,551
Total debt	5,792	6,569	6,741	7,206	4,107	3,892	4,423	4,532	4,390
Res. for deprec.	1,091	1,542	1,942	1,975	1,948	1,993	2,037	2,145	2,250
Net worth	13,309	11,569	10,411	9,581	11,799	11,517	11,272	11,108	11,050
Total	$20,192	$19,680	$19,094	$18,762	$17,854	$17,402	$17,732	$17,785	$17,690
Cash gain	$	$ 26	$	$	$	$	$	$ 227	$ 353
Depreciation	77	156	77	30	34	43	44	120	119
Net income								107	234

* Last statement before 13b loan was advanced. A Includes 13b loan-current. B Deferred 13b loan.

CASE D

(In thousands)

	9/30/32	9/30/34	9/30/35	9/30/36 *	9/30/37	6/30/38
Cash	$ 4	$ 6	$ 10	$ 16	$ 1	$ 10
Receivables	76	62	98	167	(A)304	(C)210
Inventory	71	91	112	135	300	228
Total cur. assets	151	159	220	318	605	448
Plant	100	113	127	74	109	110
Other assets	95	103	94	124	140	175
Total	$346	$375	$441	$516	$854	$733
Due banks		2	7	27	(B) 68	(D)228
Due trade	81	65	77	68	126	167
Accruals & reserves	6	12	12	12	22	46
Misc. liab.	20	28	48	87	(A)258	(C)203
Total cur. liab.	107	107	144	194	474	644
Deferred liab.					(B) 13	4
Total debt	107	107	144	194	487	648
Res. for deprec.	34	46	52	26	31	36
Net worth	205	222	245	296	336	49
Total	$346	$375	$441	$516	$854	$733
	12 Mos.	*12 Mos.*	*12 Mos.*	*12 Mos.*	*12 Mos.*	*Combined 9 Mos.*
Cash gain	$	$ 16	$ 29	$ 28	$ 25	$
Depreciation	5	6	6	7	5	9
Net income		10	23	21	20	
			(A) Includes $175M Notes Sold to Finance Company	(B) Includes $42M 13b loan of which $9M is deferred	(C) Includes $132M Notes Sold to Finance Company	(D) Includes $42M 13b loan

* Last statement before 13b loan granted.

CASE E

(*In thousands*)

	12/31/30	12/31/32	12/31/34 *	12/31/35	12/31/36	12/31/37	6/30/38
Cash	$ 6	$ 4	$ 2	$ 2	$ 1	$	$
Receivables	30	18	29	33	35	31	20
Inventory	49	28	39	40	33	35	31
Total cur. assets	85	50	70	75	69	66	51
Plant	111	113	115	123	126	130	131
Other assets	64	30	4	4	4	5	5
Total	$260	$193	$189	$202	$199	$201	$187
Due banks	3	5		10 †	10 †	8 †	5 †
" trade	1	4	11	16	14	22	20
Other liabs.			5	2	5	8	7
Total cur. liabs.	4	9	16	28	29	38	32
Deferred liab.				17 †	7 †		
Mortgage			4				
Total debt	4	9	20	45	36	38	32
Reserve for deprec.	50	61	44	49	55	61	64
Net worth	206	123	125	108	108	102	91
Total	$260	$193	$189	$202	$199	$201	$187
	12 Mos.	*12 Mos.*	*12 Mos.*	*12 Mos.*	*12 Mos.*	*12 Mos.*	*6 Mos.*
Cash gain	$ 2	$	$ 11	$	$ 4	$ 1	$
Depreciation	6	6	4	5	5	6	3
Net income			7				

* Last statement before 13b loan advanced.

† 13b loan.

CASE F

(In thousands)

	12/31/30	12/31/32	12/31/33 *	12/31/34	12/31/35	12/31/36	12/31/37	11/30/38
Cash	$ 128	$ 56	$ 84	$ 313	$ 65	$ 77	$ 40	$ 58
Receivables	1,456	857	666	611	575	554	378	211
Inventory	1,044	813	645	605	610	654	531	423
Total cur. assets	2,628	1,726	1,395	1,529	1,250	1,285	949	692
Plant	1,096	1,111	1,113	1,118	1,138	1,154	1,163	1,162
Other assets	240	273	274	273	236	264	140	72
Total	$3,964	$3,110	$2,782	$2,920	$2,624	$2,703	$2,252	$1,926
Due banks	170	293	384		(A)100	(A)325	(A)485	(A)657
Notes & drafts disc.	1,188	745	559	498	365	425	272	103
Due trade	166	47	116	136	97	136	49	27
Accruals & res.	26	37	26	13	8	4	20	23
Misc. liab.	110	125	44	45	32	32	26	22
Total cur. liabs.	1,660	1,247	1,129	692	602	922	852	832
13b loan def'd				700	600	400	200	
Total debt	1,660	1,247	1,129	1,392	1,202	1,322	1,052	832
Res. for deprec.	204	271	301	332	363	394	425	452
Net worth	2,100	1,592	1,352	1,196	1,059	987	775	642
Total	$3,964	$3,110	$2,782	$2,920	$2,624	$2,703	$2,252	$1,926
	Cons. 12 Mos.	*12 Mos.*	*12 Mos.*	*12 Mos.*	*12 Mos.*	*12 Mos.*	*12 Mos.*	*11 Mos.*
Cash gain	$ 145	$	$	$	$	$	$	$
Depreciation	40	42	40	36	37	37	37	33
Net income	105							
					(A) Current portion of 13b loan	(A) Includes $275M 13b loan	(A) Includes $460M 13b loan	(A) 13b loan

* Last statement before 13b loan granted.

Donald S. Thompson [1]

Deposit Insurance and Bank Supervision

THE DEVELOPMENT of bank supervision and of deposit insurance reflects efforts on the part of the public to secure safety and stability in their financial relationships, and assurance that the obligations of banks will be met with reasonable certainty. The search for this security has been reflected in four developments: (1) the requirement of a pledge of special assets against particular liabilities; (2) the insurance or guaranty of bank obligations; (3) bank supervision; (4) creation of the Federal Reserve System. These four developments have not been mutually exclusive nor do they fall into consistent chronological order.

Early efforts to secure safety.—The earliest efforts to obtain security of bank obligations in the United States took the form of provisions for bank commissioners to examine commercial banks and to perform other functions similar to those of present-day supervisory agencies. Several of the New England and Middle Atlantic States appointed bank commissioners during the first three decades of the nineteenth century. Very soon afterwards proposals were made for the establishment of "safety funds," or mutual guaranty plans, or for the pledge of specific assets to assure the safety of bank notes, which at that time constituted the chief obligations of banks.

Six states—New York (1829), Vermont (1831), Indiana (1834),

[1] These remarks represent the views of the author as an individual and are not to be taken as a statement of the official policy or the attitude of the Federal Deposit Insurance Corporation, except when so indicated. The conclusions reached here are based upon research conducted by the author's colleagues, but his colleagues are not to be held responsible for the statements contained herein.

Michigan (1836), Ohio (1842), and Iowa (1858)—established safety funds, or mutual guaranty plans, for a part or all of the banks operating within those states. These plans of guaranty of bank obligations were of two types.

In New York, Vermont, and Michigan the banks made annual contributions to a "bank fund," or safety fund. In case of the failure of any of the participating banks, this fund was responsible for all debts which could not be met from liquidation of assets. In each of the three states a bank commissioner, was appointed to make examinations and to exercise other supervisory powers of the same general character as those exercised in recent years by state banking authorities.

The Indiana, Ohio, and Iowa plans of guaranty of bank obligations were of a different character. These states established banking systems which were entitled "state banks," but which were actually groups of unit banks. Each "branch" of these state banks issued its own capital stock, had its own board of directors, and distributed its earnings to its own stockholders. The central boards of these banks were in effect supervisory authorities. Their most important specific duties were to supervise note issues, to pass upon applications for the organization of branches, to examine the branches, and to assume full control of the affairs of any branch found to be in a dangerous condition.

These experiments with the guaranty of bank obligations met with varying degrees of success, but on the whole appear to have served their purpose relatively well. However, in the states which established safety funds or mutual guaranty plans, as well as in other states, there was great pressure for the establishment of "free banking," with less supervision than was entailed in the safety fund and mutual guaranty plans.

In the "free" or "independent" banking systems which were established in a large proportion of the states during the second quarter of the nineteenth century, the safety of circulating bank notes, which, as I have said, at that time constituted the chief obligations of banks, was to be secured by the pledge of assets. In most of the states the assets so selected under the system of free banking included many types of assets which proved to be subject to high degrees of risk. As a consequence, the circulating notes issued by the banks in a considerable proportion of the states were subject to substantial and varying degrees of depreciation.

Establishment of the national banking system with guaranty of circulating notes and provision for bank supervision.—The national banking system was created in part for the purpose of financing the Civil War and in part for the purpose of securing a safe, uniform circulating currency. Only United States Government securities could be pledged to secure national bank notes, and these notes were further safeguarded by guaranty of redemption by the Federal Government. Provision was also made for the examination of banks by examiners appointed by the Comptroller of the Currency, applying to the country as a whole the superior standards then to be found in the state of New York. In addition, a system of legal reserve requirements was set up, to give further assurance of the banks' safety. Imposition of a tax on state bank-note circulation led to the virtual extinguishment of the state banking systems, and those previously established guaranty systems which were still in existence were discontinued.

Movement for insurance, or guaranty, of bank deposits.—The excitement caused by the first three national bank failures and the Congressional investigation of those failures affords some evidence of the shock resulting from the realization that national banks could and did fail.[2] The panics of 1873, 1893, and 1907 revealed shortcomings in our national banking system and the inability of our system of bank supervision to prevent bank failures. The seri-

[2] First National Bank, of Attica, N.Y., for which a receiver was appointed April 14, 1865; Venango National Bank, of Franklin, Pa., receiver appointed May 1, 1866; Merchants National Bank of Washington, D.C., receiver appointed May 8, 1866. See T. P. Kane's *The Romance and Tragedy of Banking* (1922), pp. 36–45.

ousness of these failures was increased by the growing importance of deposits, the payment or redemption of which was not guaranteed, relative to the circulating notes, the payment or redemption of which was guaranteed by the Government. Widespread use of bank checks in making payments had also contributed to the rapid development of state-chartered banks, so that by the close of the nineteenth century a large proportion of the nation's banks were banks without government guaranty for any part of their obligations.

As a consequence, there was considerable agitation for insurance, or guaranty, of bank deposits. Between 1886 and 1918, seventy bills were introduced into Congress providing for the guaranty of bank deposits by a Federal Government agency. How many of these bills received serious consideration by banking and currency committees is not known. Only one, however, appears to have been reported upon favorably by such committees. In 1913 the Federal Reserve Act, as reported upon by the Senate Committee on Banking and Currency, and as passed by the Senate, contained a provision placing a part of the earnings of the Federal Reserve Banks in a depositors' guaranty fund. This provision was stricken out by the conference committee.

During the same period many proposals were made in the various states for more effective supervision over state banks and for the establishment of systems of deposit guaranty for state banks. Between 1880 and 1915 bank supervisory authorities were recreated in states which had permitted them to go out of existence or to become dormant after the establishment of the national banking system, and were organized in many of the states which had not previously established them. Between 1907 and 1918 deposit guaranty systems were created in eight states—Oklahoma (1907), Kansas (1909), Nebraska (1909), Texas (1909), Mississippi (1914), South Dakota (1915), North Dakota (1917), and Washington (1917).

Bank supervision under the Federal Reserve System.—An examination of the propaganda and literature designed to bring about banking reform during the several decades prior to the establishment of the Federal Reserve System in 1913 shows that concern for the safety of bank obligations used as currency—i. e., deposits—was prominently in the minds of the public and of proponents of banking reform. Preoccupation with the question of safety is also revealed by the preamble to the Federal Reserve Act, which provides for "elastic currency," "a means for discounting commercial paper," and for "a more effective supervision of banking in the United States." Apparently it was believed by both legislators and students of banking that an elastic currency, coupled with the ability of the banks to rediscount commercial paper under pressure and with an improvement in bank supervision, would largely eliminate bank failures. It was generally believed that panics would be impossible under the new system. The belief on the part of Congress that more effective bank supervision would be forthcoming is indicated both by the preamble to the Federal Reserve Act and to some extent by the lessened agitation for deposit insurance, or guaranty.

Perhaps it was the accident of history imposing upon the Federal Reserve Banks the burden of financing the Great War, together with the magnitude of post-war adjustments, that resulted in a shift of emphasis, in actual administration, away from bank supervision. However that may be, by 1923 or 1924 the central bank philosophy of the Federal Reserve System began to emerge, and bank supervision and bank examination, as such, were practically abandoned by the system or completely subordinated to other activities. From the middle 20's to the early 30's the Federal Reserve System conducted very few examinations, restricting most of its visits to the banks to so-called credit investigations. During part of this period the Federal Reserve Board did not even have a chief examiner. The twelve Federal reserve banks received and reviewed copies of reports of examinations of their member banks by the Comptroller of the Currency and the state authorities, but their own staffs were generally small.

The introduction of the Federal Reserve System did not change, in any significant degree, the character or effectiveness of bank supervision. During the two decades from 1913 to 1933, as in the previous three decades, bank supervision continued to be exercised by the office of the Comptroller of the Currency and by the various state banking departments, without substantial modification.

The wave of bank failures during the 1920's and the collapse of the banking system in the period from 1930 to 1933 revealed the inadequacy of bank supervision and of the central banking system, as they then existed, to provide the security which depositors of banks demanded. Agitation for the guaranty, or insurance, of bank deposits was renewed. From 1919 to May, 1933, over fifty bills for this purpose were introduced into the Congress of the United States. The Federal Deposit Insurance Corporation was created in response to the demand which these bills reflected.

Present-day structure of bank supervision.—With the creation of the Federal Deposit Insurance Corporation, there are now three Federal bank supervisory agencies and 48 state bank supervisory agencies supervising banks in the continental United States. The three Federal agencies are the Comptroller of the Currency, the Board of Governors of the Federal Reserve System, and the Federal Deposit Insurance Corporation. The Comptroller of the Currency supervises primarily national banks; the Board of Governors of the Federal Reserve System supervises primarily state banks which are members of that system; and the Federal Deposit Insurance Corporation supervises insured state banks which are not members of the Federal Reserve System. In addition to supervision by Federal agencies, all state banks which are insured, including both those which are members and those which are not members of the Federal Reserve System, are supervised by the authority of the state in which they are located. Noninsured banks are supervised by their respective state supervisory authority.[3]

Duplication in bank supervision.—There is practically no duplication between the Federal Deposit Insurance Corporation and the other Federal agencies with respect to supervisory activities, as these relate to any single subject and to any individual bank or group of banks. No other Federal bank supervisory agency issues regulations on the same subjects to the same class of banks that the Federal Deposit Insurance Corporation does, and no other Federal agency exercises supervisory power over the same class of banks with regard to those matters in which the corporation exercises such authority. There may be overlapping, but the overlapping is of the same degree as that which exists by virtue of the fact that banks have to account for their income to the Bureau of Internal Revenue, pay taxes to state tax authorities, and, in the case of many banks, submit to the authority of the Social Security Board.

The Board of Governors of the Federal Reserve System has the authority to examine national banks, but does not exercise it. The Federal Deposit Insurance Corporation has authority to examine national banks only with the express consent of the Comptroller of the Currency, and state banks which are members of the Federal Reserve System only with the express consent of the Board of Governors of that System. As a consequence, there is practically no duplication in the examinations conducted by the Federal agencies.

From its inception to the close of 1938, the Federal Deposit Insurance Corporation conducted approximately 50,000 examinations, of which 110 were examinations of 100 national banks and state banks which were members of the Federal Reserve System. These 100 banks were examined for the following purposes:

[3] The Reconstruction Finance Corporation is not listed as a bank supervisory agency because its relationships with the banks grow out of its subscription to capital and partake more of the nature of the relationship between a bank and an important stockholder than between a bank and a supervisory authority. Furthermore, the Re-

1. To determine eligibility for insurance of state banks which were members of the Federal Reserve System, and which were filing notice of intention to withdraw from the Federal Reserve System and filing application for admission to insurance as banks not members of the Federal Reserve System; and of national banks seeking to convert into state banks and filing application for admission to insurance as banks not members of the Federal Reserve System, 78 banks;

2. To determine the applicability of law to proposals for mergers with the financial aid of the Federal Deposit Insurance Corporation and to appraise assets for the purpose of making loans, 8 banks;

3. To conduct proceedings for the termination of insurance status of banks engaged in unsafe and unsound practices, 14 banks.

The cost of these 110 examinations—estimated roughly at $20,000—was borne by the Federal Deposit Insurance Corporation and no part assessed against the banks.

There is duplication between the Federal establishment and the state authorities with regard to supervision of those state banks which are members of the Federal Reserve System and those which are not members of that system but which are insured. In so far as the Federal Deposit Insurance Corporation is concerned, the effects of this duplication have been lessened by arrangements for joint examinations and alternate examinations, so that in the case of insured state banks which are not members of the Federal Reserve System, the burden of examination upon these banks is little if any greater than that upon the national banks, which are examined twice each year. The direct cost to the banks is less, owing to the practice of the Federal Deposit Insurance Corporation of bearing the expense of its examinations.

Development of bank supervision empirical.—The history of bank supervision shows that its development was a phase of our demand for safety and soundness in our banking structure, and did not grow out of any considered theory nor principle of the relation

---

construction Finance Corporation does not now examine regularly any bank examined by any of the three Federal bank supervisory agencies.

of government to business, nor out of any theory of social control of business. The development was wholly empirical.

Bank supervision is not analogous to the supervision and control of public utilities. The essence of the public utility is the legal recognition of the existence and the necessary continuance of an essentially monopolistic situation. Supervision in our banking system assumes, at least in principle, the existence of a competitive situation. The prime duty of the supervisors of public utilities is to prevent the public utilities from charging monopoly prices and from discriminating against customers. Except for general usury laws, the control of interest rates charged by banks has been chiefly a relatively recent development of central-bank money market control, exercised not for the purpose of maintaining fair charges but for the purpose of maintaining general economic stability through influencing the cost of money. At times it may be the aim of the central bank to raise the cost of money so high as to ward off customers' demands for credit. It does not appear that discouraging customers' demands has ever been an object of public-utility regulation. Public utilities have generally been required to do business with all comers who are prepared to abide by the publicly supervised rules. Banks have the unreviewed right to refuse to serve individual members of the community.

Neither did bank supervision develop as an instrument of monetary control. As I have pointed out elsewhere, when the Federal Reserve System developed its central banking philosophy it practically abandoned, or at least greatly subordinated, its supervisory activities.

On the whole, I think it fair to say that bank supervision has developed with a view to assuring soundness in our individual institutions, with a minimum of interference with the conduct of the banking business.

The Federal Deposit Insurance Corporation and the need for an appraisal of bank supervision.—A survey of the systems of insurance, or guaranty, of bank obligations which had been in operation prior to the inauguration of Federal insurance, indicates that certain conditions are necessary if insurance is to provide the safety sought by depositors. These conditions may be enumerated briefly as follows:

1. Funds available must be sufficient to pay losses. If these funds are obtained by assessment, the rate must be approximately equal to the rate of loss, over a long period of time. The annual rate of assessment is about one-third the annual rate of losses to depositors, over the seventy-year period preceding the establishment of the corporation. If the corporation is to provide the safety desired, therefore, the rate of loss from failures must be lower than in the past or else additional funds must be obtained.

2. Risk must not be concentrated in one section of the country or in a few very large banks.

3. The insuring organization must have the power to establish and to maintain specified conditions of admission and bank operation, so that it will not be forced to insure abnormal risks. The corporation has the power to establish and does maintain specified conditions of admission to insurance, of banks which are not members of the Federal Reserve System. It has no such power with respect to banks which are members of the Federal Reserve System, but must insure any national bank chartered by the Comptroller of the Currency and any bank admitted to membership in the Federal Reserve System. As a matter of practice, however, the Comptroller refers all applications for national bank charters to the corporation for a statement of the corporation's opinion or attitude with regard to the granting of such charters. While the Comptroller is not bound by the recommendation of the corporation, that recommendation does carry weight in the granting of charters. Similarly, the Federal Reserve System as a general practice does not admit to membership banks which could not qualify for insurance under the standards set up by the corporation.

4. Stockholders must take a reasonable share of the risks by providing adequate capital funds. The average ratio of total capital to total assets has declined substantially during the past seventy-five years, and since the World War has averaged less than in any previous period.

5. The insured banks must be kept in a sound condition, so that the probability of an excessive number of failures in times of business depression may be reduced. Prompt supervisory action must be taken to close or to eliminate from insurance banks the condition of which becomes unsound and which cannot be rehabilitated during relatively prosperous times.

6. Adequate rediscount facilities must be available to the banks, to enable them to convert sound assets into cash when necessary. This point will be spoken of later.

The Federal Deposit Insurance Corporation was faced with a 70-year record of banking of a character which made essential a reëxamination and appraisal of supervisory principles and procedure. Over the past 70 to 75 years, the banking system as a whole has had to absorb $14,000,000,000 of losses. Of these losses, approximately $2,500,000,000 were losses of depositors, approximately $2,500,000,000 were lost by stockholders through assessments or contributions in the case of suspended or reorganized banks, and more than $9,000,000,000 were written off by active banks in the course of their operations. We do not know how much was lost through unrecorded voluntary contributions.

The ability of our banking system to continue to function as private enterprise is dependent upon its ability to absorb these losses. Bank supervision must be concerned not alone with the losses to depositors, but with the nature and origin of the $14,000,000,000 of losses sustained by the banks. If, as has sometimes been proposed, bank supervision should be divorced from the corporation and either weakened or directed to purposes other than the maintenance of sound banks, we should probably have to establish insurance reserves and an annual income sufficient to pay losses not in terms of $2,000,000,000 to $3,000,000,000 over a period of 75 years, but of substantially higher amounts and proportions.

Supervisory policy and the post-war banking crises.—In reviewing the causes of the failure of our supervisory and our central banking authorities to cope with the situation that developed in the 30's, I have reached the conclusion that if any blame is to be attached to either of them for that debacle, it is because of the adherence by each to the commercial loan theory of banking. While this theory had some historic basis for its existence, it was not descriptive of our banking system as it actually functioned in the 20's and the 30's. Bank supervisors classified and valued assets on the basis of concepts revolving around self-liquidating commercial loans, liquid open-market paper, and liquid short-term securities. These constituted a relatively small proportion of bank assets, and they, as well as other assets, did not prove to be liquidable in the markets as they existed in the 30's. With non-liquid assets, the banks were unable to meet the deposit withdrawals to which they were subjected. The banks' final recourse was to the central bank, which was operating under the same basic philosophy and was unable to provide the convertibility which the banking system needed.

Whether or not greater flexibility in our banking system would have prevented the debacle cannot be determined. It does appear, however, that the collapse of the banking system in 1933 resulted rather from the inability of banks to rediscount assets in order to meet withdrawals than from the pressure of bank supervisors for liquidation.

Development of supervisory standards under the Federal Deposit Insurance Corporation.—The early work of the Corporation revealed the existence of lack of coördination in standards and activities of the Federal and state bank supervisory authorities. Such coördination appeared to be essential to the smooth functioning of our banking system and of our supervisory and deposit insurance systems.

Following a number of conferences between representatives of the Federal Deposit Insurance Corporation and the Executive Committee of the National Association of Supervisors of state banks, that committee, on April 15, 1938, adopted or endorsed certain principles and procedures governing examinations of banks, and recommended their adoption by the various state authorities. The Corporation agreed to these recommendations and advised the other Federal bank supervisory agencies of its intention of putting them into effect. By the summer of 1938, general agreement was obtained among the Federal agencies in Washington. The principles and procedures finally adopted as standard in the summer of 1938 by all the Federal agencies in Washington and most of the state authorities were substantially similar to those endorsed by the state supervisors earlier in the year.

Principles underlying current supervisory standards.—The basic principles underlying the standard examination procedure may be summarized as follows:

1. The banks' affairs should be so conducted as to insure the ability of the banks to meet their customers' demands and to serve the legitimate credit needs of their communities.

2. Bank liquidity is dependent not so much upon the actual liquidation of assets through sale in open markets or through maturity and retirement of obligations held, as upon the transfer of sound assets from banks under pressure to banks not under pressure, or to other institutions.

3. The criterion in appraising the quality of assets is not maturity, but soundness in terms of the ability of the obligor to service his obligation and to meet his contract.

4. It is tacitly assumed that the central bank will rediscount assets, not on the basis of maturity and the conformability of the paper to so-called commercial-loan standards, but on the basis of

the soundness of the assets as measured by the ability of the obligors to meet the terms of their contracts; and that it will rediscount these assets on the basis of reasonable appraised values, rather than that of current market values.

These principles represent the application to bank supervisory practices and to central banking operations of the principles embodied in the Banking Act of 1935 and in the revised Regulation A of the Board of Governors of the Federal Reserve System.

In so far as the Federal Deposit Insurance Corporation was concerned, these principles had been applied to the appraisal of loans since the joint examiners' conference held in Washington in September, 1934.

Limitations on bank examinations and bank supervision.—It is the task of the supervisor to establish the general policies governing the examiners' work, to develop rules and standards of sound banking, and to determine what corrective measures, if any, should be adopted in individual cases. It is the work of the examiner to appraise the assets of the bank, to determine the capital position of the bank, to check the conformity of the bank's operations with law and regulation, and to assist in the development of corrective programs when necessary.

Appraisal of assets requires skill and judgment on the part of the examiner, to be acquired only by training and experience. The examiner deals with particular cases, in individual loans. He works under considerable pressure and has little or no opportunity to sit back and view the scene in broad perspective. Therefore, he must be supplied with standards to be used as guides in making his appraisals and in analyzing the position of the bank. These standards must be relatively simple and objective, since the examiner cannot be expected to vary his application of them with changes in economic conditions nor to exert pressure for expansion nor restriction of credit. Dealing with individual cases, as he does, his efforts at credit control will impinge, let us say, upon the extension of a loan to John Jones. Substitution of the judgment of an examiner or of a low-salaried government official for that of the banker in extending individual loans and lines of credit does not provide a solution of the problem of economic instability. It is also incompatible with a system of private enterprise. Bank supervision cannot be substituted for bank management, but can serve only as a check on ill-conceived or unethical banking practices and policies. The examiner and the supervisor can insist only that credit extensions shall be on a reasonably sound and disinterested basis, and that individual banks shall not expose themselves to undue concentration of risk. A reasonably sound basis is one which provides reasonable assurance that the obligor can service his obligation. A disinterested basis is one which assures that the banker will deal with his customers impersonally and will not try to act in a dual capacity.

Just as the central banking system should operate with some flexibility, so is it desirable to have some flexibility in supervisory policy, as expressed in the review of examinations made and the programs of correction determined upon. It is important that the supervisor should guard against optimism in times of business prosperity and against pessimism in times of business depression. Supervisors should not insist upon the liquidation of criticized assets during periods of depression nor financial strain. Sound banking policy and sound supervisory policy require the setting aside each year of part of the income, to take care of any losses, and the prompt writing off of any losses as they occur or as they may be ascertained. Such policy may be effected through the use of valuation allowances or through other accounting procedures, rather than by forced liquidation or sale of assets. The present policy of the Corporation is to require banks to recognize their losses by adjustments in their accounts, and to leave actual liquidation of the assets to the discretion of the bankers, except when violations of law are involved.

In the past most of the banks' losses have been incurred through liquidation under adverse economic pressure, forced by deposit withdrawals and by inadequate rediscount facilities. If the central banking system does not adhere, in the future, to the principle of rediscounting sound assets at reasonable values, the commercial banks will not be able to meet demands under severe strain, and our improved supervisory standards will not have contributed to stability to any significant degree.

Deposit Insurance as a stabilizing factor.—At the present time insurance coverage is limited to a maximum of $5,000 for each depositor. This covers more than 98 percent of the accounts in the banks, but only 45 percent of the deposits. If the primary purpose of deposit insurance is to aid in providing security for the masses of the population with small and moderate incomes, then the $5,000 limitation is adequate. If, however, the primary aim of deposit insurance is to protect the country's customary means of payment and to guarantee it against shrinkage as a result of runs and bank failures, then the limitation of insurance coverage to $5,000 is not adequate. Nearly three-fourths of the demand deposits of individuals and business enterprises are in accounts with balances of more than $5,000, and it is these balances which are used in making the bulk of the payments involved in production and trade.

In small communities, where the banks are small and the insurance coverage under the $5,000 limitation is very high, the present law does provide nearly complete protection of the active currency of the community. In the industrial centers and large cities, however, which are dependent for their currency upon the large banks and the accounts of large business enterprises, the present limitation provides only meager protection for the community's circulating medium.

The protection afforded deposits in large accounts, however, actually is considerably greater than would be indicated by the $5,000 limitation. This is due to two factors: (1) the fact that many holders of deposits with balances above $5,000 are either protected by pledge of security or legal preference, or become aware that a bank is in difficulties and draw out their deposits prior to suspension; and (2) the tradition of some years' standing, intensified by experience in the recent crisis, that the government cannot afford to permit any large bank to fail. The protection provided in this way, however, is uncertain and may not prevent the stress of a period of business recession from generating a banking panic, with its disastrous effects upon the volume of production and upon the flow of income in the community.

Elimination of bank runs.—It has long been believed that many bank suspensions are caused by rumors spread among depositors, and that many banks in sound condition have thus been forced to close because of runs. It is assumed, furthermore, that such runs are made primarily by a large number of holders of small accounts, who are not acquainted with the character of the bank management and who for this reason are especially susceptible to the influence of rumors. Deposit insurance, even when limited to $5,000 for each depositor, should eliminate such runs, and has, in fact, already done so, in so far as the appearance of long lines of people waiting at the doors of a bank is concerned.

However, an analysis of deposits in closed banks, made by the Board of Governors of the Federal Reserve System, indicates that it is primarily the holders of large accounts, rather than the holders of small accounts, who withdraw their deposits most rapidly when loss of confidence occurs. Withdrawals of deposits by the holders of large accounts are less spectacular than those by the holders of small accounts, since they are made by drawing checks for deposit in another bank or, more probably, merely by depositing current receipts in a new account in another bank and paying current expenses from the old account. It is only when adverse clearing-house balances accumulate that the officials of banks realize that a "silent run" is in progress.

Extension of deposit insurance to cover all liabilities.—Bank failures may be attributed primarily to one of the two following general factors, or to a combination of the two: first, internal factors, such as mismanagement and defalcation; and secondly, external factors, such as adverse business conditions, resulting in the inability of borrowers from banks to meet their obligations and in the withdrawal of balances to meet payments due in other parts of the country. If a bank is in difficulties because of mismanagement, the holders of large accounts usually know something about the situation prior to the time when the bank is forced to close, and tend to draw down their deposit accounts to the $5,000 balance which is insured. If a bank is in difficulties because of adverse business conditions in the community in which it operates, it is likely to suffer an unfavorable balance of payments, owing to the fact that depositors are using their balances to pay for supplies purchased from other sections of the country.

When deposit withdrawals occur, regardless of whether they are due to the depositors' fear that the bank is incapably managed or to the necessity which depositors face of making payments in other parts of the country, the banks from which the withdrawals are made find it necessary either to dispose of assets or to borrow and to pledge assets as collateral for such borrowings. Borrowing or disposal of assets, however, becomes difficult in times of regional or national business depression, when adverse economic circumstances are affecting the value and the saleability of the assets owned by the banks. The market situation which makes it difficult to sell assets and thus induces borrowing by the banks, also makes it necessary for the banks to pledge to support such borrowing collateral in amounts far in excess of the amounts borrowed.

The insuring of all direct liabilities of the banks would increase the ability of banks to liquidate assets by transferring them to other banks or to the central bank. The insurance of the Corporation would afford protection to the lending institution. Such extension of the insurance principle would increase confidence in the workability of the assumption upon which our entire supervisory and central banking policies are based, namely, that liquidity of bank assets is to be found not in their disposal in the open market nor in the enforced liquidation of borrowers, but in the transfer of sound assets from institutions which need cash to institutions with excess cash resources, or to the central bank.

The extension of insurance to cover all liabilities of banks raises certain questions and problems. Full insurance will maintain confidence in the banking system only if confidence is felt in the ability of the Federal Deposit Insurance Corporation to fulfill its obligations. As of December 31, 1938, the total capital account of the Corporation amounted to $402,000,000. In addition, the Corporation has a borrowing power of approximately $1,000,000,000. The total funds available to the Corporation, therefore, are about $1,500,000,000. As previously pointed out, the assessment rate is low. The capital position of the banks is weaker than ever before. Although our banking system has been established with a view to increasing its flexibility and its ability to convert assets into cash under strain, the system has not yet been put to the test. Furthermore, it is not known what the effect upon our business and financial practices may be, psychologically or otherwise, of the increased bearing of risk by an agency of the Federal Government. One thing is true; if the Corporation or any other agency were to assume all of the banking risks which management and private ownership are unable to assume, the authority of that Corporation or agency would have to be extended and strengthened. A strict policy would have to be instituted of moving promptly, except during periods of adverse economic conditions, to eliminate from insurance, or to liquidate, or to reorganize any bank which fell below a certain minimum standard of condition, as determined by its capital ratio and the quality of its assets.

Cost of increased insurance coverage.—The experience of the

Corporation to date does not indicate that increased coverage would raise the cost of insurance materially.

Bank deposits are given protection at the present time to a far greater degree than is commonly realized. In the insolvent insured banks which have been placed in receivership, or reorganized and merged with the financial aid of the Federal Deposit Insurance Corporation, deposits were protected to the following extent:

Year	*Percent*
1935	85.2
1936	93.4
1937	98.2
1938	99.6

Surveying the situation as we know it to exist, it does not appear that the coverage will be much lower in the insolvent banks which will have closed or merged by the end of 1939.

In periods of depression banks will have borrowed heavily and will have pledged substantial amounts of their sound assets to secure such borrowing. The pledged assets, therefore, will not be available to protect the remaining depositors and the Federal Deposit Insurance Corporation from loss in the event of failure. To insure against loss the borrowings which would otherwise be protected by the pledge of assets, therefore, would not materially increase the losses of the Corporation. On the contrary, complete control of the assets of the insolvent bank should permit the Corporation, as sole creditor, to liquidate the assets under the most favorable circumstances, thus securing maximum returns. Receivership costs should also be reduced.

Branch banking as a factor in stability.—Supervision is an attempt to obtain assurance that the banks' affairs are properly and honestly managed and that the banks are kept in a sound condition. The existence of deposit insurance is a recognition of the fallibility of human judgments and institutions, with their consequent more or less occasional failures.

One suggestion for reducing or eliminating bank failures is the extension of branch banking on a nation-wide scale or at least on a broad geographic scale, with relatively few large banks controlling the banking resources of the country. It is claimed that in this way risks would be diversified, strain of adverse balance of payments materially reduced, if not eliminated, and more competent management secured. Many studies have been made attesting the shortcomings of our numerous small, weak, and independent banks and the virtues and strength of our large banks. Many of the studies have concluded that an extension of the geographic scope of branch banking is the proper solution of our banking difficulties. The merits or demerits of branch banking will not be discussed here, but a review of the results of some of the investigations into the basic assumptions underlying most discussions of branch banking should be of interest.

Large versus small banks.—When Federal insurance of deposits became effective in 1934, more than 7,000 banks which were not members of the Federal Reserve System were insured. These were in general, the small banks of the country. More than half of them had deposits of less than $250,000 each. Seven-eighths of them had deposits of less than $1,000,000 each. If the small bank was inherently weak and uneconomic, here was a real problem. The energies and resources of the Corporation were devoted to the study of the problem and to devising programs for strengthening or eliminating these weak, uneconomic institutions. Findings to date may be summarized as follows:

1. The small banks have a better capital position than the large.

2. The quality of the assets of the small banks appears to be on a par with the quality of the assets of the large banks.

3. The small banks have maintained a higher proportion of their assets in loans than have the large banks.

4. The small banks show consistently better net earnings, in terms of assets, than do the large banks.

5. In the performance of their particular tasks, the managements of the small banks do not appear to be sufficiently inferior to the managements of the large banks to give any great cause for concern.

6. The rates of losses sustained on loans and on securities by operating national banks over a period of twenty years (1918–37) have been no higher for country banks than for city banks.

7. The small banks have not had the rediscount and borrowing facilities of the large banks, owing in part to their inability to operate as easily as the large banks in accordance with the principles of the commercial-loan theory of banking, and in part to their inability or refusal to join the Federal Reserve System and to the inability of the Federal Reserve System to make its facilities available to the many small nonmember banks. The shortcomings in the rediscount facilities of the Federal Reserve System, which arose from an adherence by that system to the commercial-loan theory of banking, have already been pointed out.

8. In the past, supervisory standards appear to have been applied more strictly to the small banks than to the large banks, so that weak, small banks were closed more promptly than were large banks in a comparable condition.

9. A higher proportion of small banks than of large banks has failed. However, the difference was at least partly due to the heroic efforts of government agencies to keep the large banks from failing, and partly to the fact that banks in agricultural regions—the smaller banks—were under severe adverse pressure for thirteen years, while the banks in industrial, commercial, and financial regions—the larger banks—were subject to pressure for less than two years in the early 20's and for only three years in the early 30's. Studies are now under way to appraise, among other factors, the extent of failures of banks of different sizes, when located in similar geographic and economic areas, in places of comparable size and economic characteristics, and when subject to approximately similar

competitive situations. These studies have not yet been completed. The results should prove interesting.

10. The embarrassment of a few large banks, through adverse circumstances, could involve greater loss to the Corporation and to the public and could contribute more to the instability of our economic institutions than the suspension of all of the so-called weak, uneconomic, small banks, combined.

Branch banks versus unit banks.—Returning to the question of branch banking, our findings indicate the following:

1. The capital ratios of the branch systems are lower than those of the unit banks.

2. The proportion of substandard assets is higher in the branch banks than in the unit banks.

3. Branch banks show lower net earnings per $100 of assets than do the unit banks.

4. The managements of branch banks do not appear to be superior to those of the unit banks.

5. Sufficient evidence has not been presented to support the contention that branches are operated more economically than are unit banks of comparable size.

Many of the branch banks, the data for which were included in our study, are relatively small banks, while others are those restricted to city-wide operation. Further analysis of the findings is necessary, therefore, before they can be accepted. The only purpose in raising the question here is to indicate that the case for branch banking has by no means been proved.

Conclusion.—Deposit insurance and bank supervision reflect an effort to secure safety for depositors and effectiveness in the operations of our banks. Whether consciously or not, they also represent an effort on the part of the public to preserve, through the pooling of depositors' risks, the best features of our system of a large number of independent banks. The purpose of deposit insurance is to avoid or minimize losses to depositors. The purpose of bank supervision is to keep banks sound. These objectives can be achieved, but not without effort.

The rate of assessment for insurance is about one-third the rate of losses experienced by depositors over a seventy-year period. The rate of losses must be kept at a level greatly reduced from that of the past, if safety through a self-supporting insurance system is to be maintained. A reduced rate of losses can be secured only through sound banking and through an effectively functioning central banking system. Our traditions indicate that soundness can be achieved only through correct management and proper supervision. If supervision is weakened or turned from its basic purpose of maintaining a sound condition, it will be necessary to obtain additional funds in order to be prepared to meet losses, which on the basis of past experience may average considerably higher than the present rate of assessment. If the bankers and the depositors are not prepared to meet this cost, effective supervision must be maintained, or the United States Treasury must bear the financial burden, in effect giving subsidy and relief to the bankers, even as these are given to the farmers and to those on relief. To attempt to weaken our system of deposit insurance and bank supervision, without recognizing the need, and making adequate provision in advance, for the assumption of financial responsibility, is to invite the ultimate socialization of banking in this country. However, the most skillfully administered system of deposit insurance and the most admirable plan for bank supervision cannot prevent a collapse of our banking system, in the absence of an effectively functioning central bank.

Amos E. Taylor

Methods in the Preparation of the Balance of International Payments of the United States

I FEEL somewhat embarrassed at the thought of defining the term "balance of payments." I am going to avoid doing so—at least for the moment. About six months ago I received a letter from a student at Smith College, in which the young lady told me at length that she was interested in preparing a Senior term paper on some phase of the balance of international payments, and requested that I tell her what is meant by a balance of international payments. I thought that the best kind of service I could perform was to send her without charge a copy of our latest annual bulletin, which I felt contained a clear explanation. About three weeks later I received a reply, in which the young lady indicated that she had definitely decided to write her paper on the balance of international payments, and then added: "Would you mind preparing for me a brief statement on just what the balance of international payments is? I have read your bulletin."

Of course a number of individual items, each relating to a particular transaction, are involved in the definition of the term. I shall therefore not attempt to lay down a specific definition. It is frequently said that in preparing an international balance we simply set over against one another the various international transactions which in some way affect foreign exchange operations. In fact, however, many international transactions do not really affect the foreign exchanges. We often find it necessary to enter transactions which do not involve payments. A common example is found in gifts which are sent out of the country in the form of merchandise, which, in many cases, may be included in the reported trade exports. It may be said that in principle such a merchandise item should be excluded from the trade figures reported in the balance of payments. In practice this might force us to take something which cannot be identified out of the recorded figures, and it may be thus statistically desirable not to eliminate it but to have it offset by an equivalent item somewhere on the other side of the statement. We may take, for example, gifts sent abroad in the form of merchandise by charitable, religious, or other institutions. If we consider all reported contributions of this kind received in this country as invisible imports, they will presumably include the necessary offset to those recorded merchandise exports which have been shipped abroad as gifts. Because of the various difficulties involved in making these distinctions, I shall confine myself primarily to transactions as distinct from actual payments. It was agreed only recently by a special Balance-of-Payments Subcommittee of the League of Nations, of which I am a member, that the emphasis in the presentation of individual items in the preparation of balance-of-payments statements should be placed on transactions rather than on payments. I think this is a correct view, and it should be emphasized.

It might be well for me to outline the methods followed in collecting and compiling our statistical material. Even this could easily involve us in collateral problems which would be quite worth while discussing, if time permitted. I shall attempt, however, to show just how we proceed in our statistical computations. In order to do this as conveniently as possible, I think I might simply go down the line and discuss each of the various classes of transactions in order.

In the beginning I want to refer briefly to our merchandise trade, which is the most important item in our international business. Our export and import trade is, of course, officially reported in some detail every month. In preparing the statement on the balance of payments, we take these trade figures for the year as a whole or for whatever period the statement may cover, and first record the totals as officially reported by our Division of Foreign Trade Statistics. Under a separate heading we incorporate the results of various corrections and adjustments, with the result that the final statement will represent as closely as possible the actual dollar receipts or payments. It must be remembered that our foreign-trade statistics have developed largely as a by-product of fiscal administration. It is important that duties on dutiable goods be collected, and that the recorded entries reflect correct valuation. Many commodities, however, are not subject to duty, while many others are subject to specific duties. Even in the case of imports subject to ad valorem duties, it may happen (especially in periods of unstable currencies) that the value for duty purposes does not accurately represent the dollar cost to the importer. Reference to these factors implies no criticism of our official trade statistics. It must be borne in mind that the primary compilation of these figures cannot necessarily be shown at once in final form for balance-of-payments purposes.

We also find that there are certain transactions which for obvious reasons are not included in our ordinary export-import statistics. An example is to be found in the sale and purchase of ships. It may happen that a wealthy American decides to have a yacht built, for example, at Kiel; that is, of course, a form of commodity purchase, and must be taken into account somewhere in the aggregate of our international transactions. Sales and purchases of coal and oil for bunker purposes also represent international commodity transactions which are not included in our official foreign trade figures. On the other hand, certain items are included in the reported figures of exports and imports which in no way involve payments, as for example household goods accompanying persons entering the United States or persons departing from this country.

For a number of years a very interesting item included in this special type of merchandise trade was smuggled liquor. At first the estimate covering the value of this contraband commodity was shown separately in the international balance, but it presented so many possibilities of dramatic presentation, and consequently of misrepresentation of the balance of payments as a whole, that the estimated value was subsequently included with a number of miscellaneous transactions. There are, of course, other types of contraband articles, such as drugs and narcotics, for which allowance must be made.

Another problem in this general category which is being explored at the present time relates to the "payments" value of our merchandise imports. Under our Tariff Act and customs regulations, merchandise imports are supposed to be entered at the f.o.b. value at the foreign point of shipment. If we assume that our import values are correctly entered, we have to include in the balance of payments a separate estimate covering freight payments to foreign steamship lines, as well as cargo insurance payments made to foreign companies. It follows, therefore, that if at any time freight and insurance are by chance included in the official trade figures, our balance-of-payments statement would contain certain duplications. With a view to exploring the problem of import entries, we undertook about a year ago to examine several hundred thousand invoices and entry records, through the means of a special WPA project. We were especially interested in studying the import statistics of such commodities as rubber, silk, coffee, oil, and copper. We were interested not simply in seeing whether in practice any of these entries might possibly be on a c.i.f. basis, but we also wanted to know more about the conditions under which imported commodities originating from American-owned properties abroad were shipped and marketed. The reason for the latter type of inquiry lies in the fact that the recorded value of such imports may in substantial part represent earnings or working capital funds, which do not enter into offsetting payments made abroad. It is thus obvious that there is a connection between our merchandise import data and our estimate (on the opposite side of the international balance) of dividend receipts on so-called direct investments in foreign countries. Our study of these problems has not proceeded far enough to make possible the presentation of any definite conclusions. I believe that I have shown, however, that in preparing the statement on the balance of payments, we need to make certain additions to, deductions from, and other adjustments of, the official foreign trade figures. As already indicated, we follow the convenient procedure of simply entering the official foreign trade figures as reported, and then making the various corrections and changes in a separate item. It is believed undesirable to enter the combined foreign trade statistics and adjustment estimates in a single item, because of the inevitable confusion that would arise from the official publication of two sets of figures, each purporting to show the value of the year's merchandise exports and imports.

We have a form of invisible trade, represented by the freight and shipping services, which is somewhat unusual in character because of the manner in which the merchandise export and import figures of this country are reported. In contrast with the practice of the United States and Canada in recording import values f.o.b. foreign point of shipment, most of the other important commercial countries enter such values on a c.i.f. basis. It is for this reason that, in principle, shipping expenditures in this country are not included in the official merchandise figures, and we therefore enter them as separate items. Our payments to foreign shipping lines for the carriage of American imports materially exceed the earnings of our own lines from the carriage of our exports to foreign countries. These are the only two freight items that enter into the balance of payments. In cases in which American vessels carry our own imports, the freight payment is a purely domestic payment since it involves a transaction between an American importer and an American shipping agency. Similarly, if goods exported from the United States are carried in foreign vessels, the transaction becomes one between a foreign importer and a foreign shipper. In addition to the entered estimates covering payments by American importers to foreign shipping lines and payments by foreign importers of American goods to United States ocean carriers, we also have to take account of certain railway freight items. Certain Canadian over-sea exports and imports are carried across American railways, while the two Canadian railway systems are employed in the shipment of American goods through Ontario and other parts of Canada. A small amount of similar freight service is involved in trade across the United States–Mexican border. The problem of preparing these freight estimates is frequently quite involved, and may result in somewhat inaccurate figures. For example, railways operating in Ontario may be United States owned and may be operated in such a manner that most freight payments are made to the head offices in the United States. In some of these cases equipment is repaired at termini in the United States, while crews operate across Canadian territory between two United States points. The allocation of receipts and payments under such circumstances involves technical accounting problems which increase the difficulties. The estimate relating to ocean freight and Great Lakes shipping payments are prepared for us by the Maritime Commission. This is one of the few instances in which our estimates are entirely prepared by an outside agency.

We now come to an item which has a certain amount of romance associated with it—expenditures of American tourists abroad. In the preparation of the expenditure estimates, we employ five different questionnaire forms. We secure from the Department of State a sampling of names of passport applicants, to whom questionnaire forms are submitted. We ask these travelers to indicate where they went, whether they traveled on American or foreign ships, what their expenditures were, and several other questions relating to their travel abroad. In the case of alien residents, we use as a basis for the circulation of the questionnaire form the reëntry records of the Immigration and Naturalization Service. In our canvass of United States citizens, we employ approximately 20,000 forms every year, of which we have about 25 percent returned to us with the requested information. Our distribution among the alien residents aggregates about 15,000 every year, of which the percentage returned is somewhat higher than in the case of citizens. We also employ three post-card questionnaire forms, two of which are distributed along the Canadian border. One of these forms is distributed by our border officials to American motorists coming back from Canada. In order that we may cover a representative cross section of travelers throughout the week, we have devised a system under which the distribution, at least once during each month of the year, includes travelers for every day of the week. In our sample of 25,000, we allow for a proportionately heavy distribution during the tourist season. By these methods we try to get a cross-section view of all types of travelers going to Canada. The second post-card form covers those who enter Canada by railroad or by steamship. In recent years we have had about 15,000 forms distributed to this group at the various border stations and ports. The system is not operating quite as satisfactorily as we hope it will eventually. Finally, we have a post-card questionnaire form distributed to returning motorists at the various Mexican border points. In this case the percentage of returns has been relatively high, and for reasons which are not quite clear a very high percentage of travelers seems to take advantage of the privilege given on the forms of offering special comments about the trip. Perhaps this is because automobile travel over good roads to Mexico is still somewhat of a novelty. The opening of the road between Laredo and Mexico City has encouraged motor travel through Mexico, and most of the travelers speak enthusiastically about their tour south of the Rio Grande.

Next I wish to refer briefly to another form of invisible transaction—so-called "personal" remittances as distinguished from commercial remittances. These involve more or less unilateral transactions. At times they include substantial transfers of savings from the United States to foreign countries. Until recently we almost invariably designated the item as "immigrant" remittances, on the theory that the greater part of noncommercial remittances grows out of transfers by aliens in this country to their relatives abroad. Perhaps we could appropriately continue this designation, but I believe that there is no longer any special need to place special emphasis on the word "immigrant." This class of remittances fell below $100,000,000 a year during the depression. After the war the item increased to about $500,000,000 for a few years, owing principally to the inclusion of large contributions made in this country for the purpose of feeding the hungry of Europe. During the early 1920's an attempt was made to prepare the estimates on the basis of statistics furnished by our foreign banks. Later there was an increasing tendency to secure estimates from our foreign officers abroad. For reasons beyond anyone's control, these figures were not always satisfactory, and after the inauguration of foreign exchange controls early in the depression it became increasingly difficult to get any kind of estimate from foreign sources. We are now trying to build up the annual data through the direct coöperation of American remitting agencies. In this effort we have been fairly successful. One continuing difficulty arises from the fact that no satisfactory means has yet been devised whereby we can determine what part of the international postal money-order remittances belong in this category.

Insurance is a very important element of international business, especially between Canada and the United States and between England and the United States. In exploring that field we have followed a procedure whereby the balance-of-payments entry is based on what is in fact the net transfer of funds. Insurance transactions involve capital movements, including all kinds of security transactions. They include transfers of funds from home offices to foreign branches. We consider the home office of a foreign company as a distinct domestic entity, and trace all transactions to the point where we have the net transfer of funds as a resultant. Many technical problems are involved, and because of this it was decided at Geneva last December that the question should be subjected to special study by some person or group of persons.

There are various other kinds of invisible transactions. Motion-picture royalty receipts may be cited as an example of an important invisible export. There are other items, perhaps less important, some of which show an "export" balance while others show an excess of "imports."

I should like to call special attention to dividend and interest payments. The international movement of dividend and interest items is naturally quite high. We have abroad approximately $11,000,000,000 of so-called long-term investments, of which about $4,000,000,000 is represented by what is left of the large mass of foreign dollar bonds floated in the American market during the 1920's. The remaining $7,000,000,000 is represented by so-called direct investments of American corporations in foreign properties such as plantations, petroleum properties, copper mines, branch factories, and so forth, the kind of investment which is in effect the "foreign" part of American industrial concerns and their properties. In addition to these long-term investments, we have so-called short-term holdings abroad which aggregate slightly less than $750,000,000.

On the other hand, foreigners have invested in the United States about $8,000,000,000, of which approximately $2,000,000,000 is represented by dollar balances and other short-term funds. The figure of approximately $5,700,000,000, which represents so-called "long-term" foreign investments in this country, is a somewhat heterogeneous "value aggregate" of various kinds of investments. The figure is based primarily on a special study which we made a few years ago. A substantial part of the total is represented by foreign holdings of small blocks of American corporate shares. The only feasible means for converting the share figures into dollar values is that of showing them on a market-value basis. Bonds and preferred stock were reported at par value. An additional amount of $1,500,000,000 consists of foreign direct investments in the United States. In another group we included the capitalized value of the estimated income paid out by trust funds to beneficiaries living in foreign countries. The estimated value of this group of investments was placed at roughly $450,000,000. Finally, there are estimates covering such investments as real estate, urban and agricultural mortgage bonds, and so forth.

It appears, therefore, that we have approximately $12,000,000,000 of investments abroad and close to $8,000,000,000 of foreign investments in this country. Estimated dividend and interest payments in the respective directions are not in exactly the same ratio as the investments themselves. This results from a number of factors, not the least important of which is the fact that foreign holdings in this country of approximately $2,000,000,000 consist of bank balances, the earnings on which are virtually nil.

The collection of the various classes of statistics involves the use of a number of special forms. The use of such forms extends to the preparation of estimates covering interest and dividend receipts from American direct investments abroad. In this particular work we have received excellent coöperation from the various companies concerned. The special study of a few years ago of foreign investments in the United States required considerable aid and coöperation on the part of both banks and business corporations. Since from 30 to 40 percent of foreign-held shares of American corporations are carried in the names of American nominees rather than in the names of the foreign beneficial owners, it was necessary that we secure the aid of the nominee institutions. Much of the preliminary work was accomplished through our meeting directly with representatives of the various banks in New York. The Stock Exchange also gave us considerable help in carrying the study to completion.

In our computation of interest receipts on American-held foreign dollar bonds we relied considerably on a cumulative card index of individual issues, which has constantly been kept up to date. There is, however, one difficulty which arises in connection with the preparation of the interest data, namely, that of determining what proportion of individual issues has been bought back from American holders by foreign investors or by foreign obligors. Another problem of recent years has developed from the fact that exchange controls have prevented the transfer of interest earnings from certain foreign countries. The same difficulty applies to earnings on some of our direct investments abroad.

Before concluding, I should like to refer briefly to several transactions which fall outside the groups thus far discussed. The international movements of gold and silver are, of course, a matter of record, and while we may have to make certain adjustments to cover special year-end situations, these are minor details. In the case of international security transactions, we now have the advantage of detailed figures. About the beginning of 1935 the Treasury began to collect statistics on such transactions. Until that time we had made our own estimate of international security transactions, based on an annual questionnaire form circulated among banks and brokers. Our figures were confined, of course, to the respective year ends, and we had no way of observing the nature and volume of short-term changes.

Just one more point. We are asked every now and then, What about the residual item? The figure at the bottom of our annual statement might be appropriately referred to as an annual headache. Since 1934 the estimated computed and recorded "imports" have uniformly exceeded the corresponding "exports." I do not believe that it is simply a coincidence that this has happened persistently since 1934. In 1933, although there was quite a flight of capital from the United States, the estimated balance resulted in such a small residual item that we found ourselves somewhat embarrassed. But beginning in 1934 the annual net imports of gold have exceeded $1,000,000,000 every year. Although with the exception of 1938 the net balance on account of trade and service transactions was relatively small, the net imports of gold and silver have exceeded the reported net capital inflow by a considerable margin. The policy we have followed is that of reporting what we find, on the basis of estimates prepared as scientifically as possible. There is always a temptation to make arbitrary adjustments or corrections for the sake of eliminating the residual. It is my conviction that we must guard against this and that it is better to face a troublesome and large unaccounted-for item than to face possible embarrassment later through the emergence of facts which may reflect unfavorably on the original approach. We are trying steadily to improve the estimates, both qualitatively and quantitatively. In this effort we have always been glad to receive the suggestions of those who make use of our reports.

Horace L. Sanford

The New York Money Market

I SHALL NOT attempt to cover the whole subject of the money market, nor even that of the New York money market, but shall confine my remarks to some phase or phases of money-market work.

The measurement of the flow of funds in and out of the New York money market will form the main topic of my discussion. I shall also touch on a few other points, by way of background. First of all, I should like to point out that there are some very marked differences between the money-market situation as it exists now and the situation as it was, say prior to 1933. In other words, conditions in the ten-year period 1924–33 were quite different from those of the present day.

In the first place, the supply of short-term, high-grade paper and securities at the present time is much more limited than was the case in the years prior to 1929. For example, in 1926 the total of brokers' loans was about $3,500,000,000, while at the present time it is roughly only $700,000,000. These loans constituted the principal instrument in the New York money market which was available for the short-term investment of bank funds, both of New York City institutions and also of out-of-town banks. In 1926 bankers' bills, otherwise known as acceptances, were outstanding to the approximate amount of $800,000,000. At the present time there is only about $250,000,000 of such paper outstanding. Open-market commercial paper, which was a favorite bank investment medium in 1926, was outstanding to the amount of about $650,000,000 at that time, while now the figure has fallen to $200,000,000. Treasury certificates were then outstanding to the amount of $800,000,000; today there are no such certificates outstanding. These certificates were United States Government securities of a maturity up to one year. On the other hand, we have a new type of instrument, the Treasury bill, now outstanding to the amount of $1,300,000,000. (The Treasury bill is, on the whole, a somewhat shorter-term instrument; maturities are now being sold for ninety days, although the maximum maturity possible is one year.) This is the picture as far as the supply of short-term money-market material is concerned—a reduction of approximately $3,300,000,000. The total figure is now about $2,450,000,000—indeed a sharp contraction in the supply of short-term paper and securities.

Another development that I want to mention is the accumulation at the present time of very heavy excess reserves in the banking system. In 1926, on the other hand, the banking system was borrowing a substantial amount from the Federal Reserve Banks. The change in the supply of reserves between 1926 and the present time is marked. At this time the excess reserves of all member banks are roughly $3,400,000,000. There is reason to believe that we will have an excess of $4,000,000,000 soon, and even the sum of $5,000,000,000 is in prospect. In short, we have now a heavy supply of surplus bank reserves, amounting to $3,400,000,000 for all member banks, and to virtually $2,000,000,000 for New York City banks.

The combined result of the shrinkage in the supply of short-term money market material and the very great rise in the excess reserves of the New York City banks and of all banks has been a decline in short-term money rates to very low levels indeed. I referred above to a shrinkage in the supply of short-term paper amounting to something like $3,300,000,000. There has, however, been a great increase in another type of investment medium. I refer here to the augmentation of the volume of Treasury notes and

Treasury bonds outstanding. To a considerable extent, bank funds have been invested in these longer-term Government securities, and the yield on the longer-term securities has also declined considerably. As a matter of fact, with the large increase in the supply of

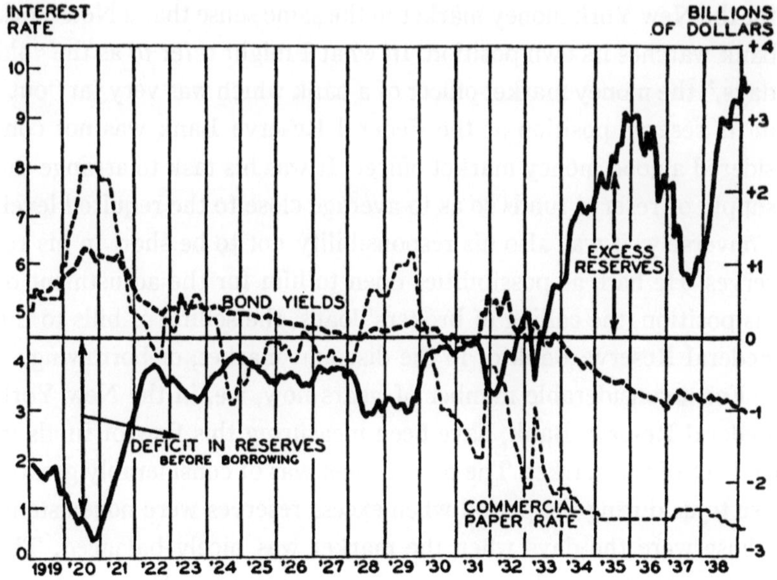

CHART I

Reserve Position of Member Banks Compared with Bond Yields and Commercial Paper Rate (Bond Yield Line Represents Moody's Investors Service data for Aaa corporation bonds)

longer-term Government securities and the heavy participation of member banks in the purchase of Government securities, it can be said that the Government security market has become the most important division of the money market. This is the situation as we now have it, an entirely different picture than we had, let us say, in 1926. Chart I shows the relation between bank reserves and money rates.

To return to my main theme, the Federal Reserve Bank of New

York makes use of report sheets, in an effort to measure the flow of funds coming into the New York money market and the movement of funds going out of the New York money market. In other words, the reserve bank is doing for the money market as a whole what each New York City bank does for itself. It is bookkeeping for the New York money market in the same sense that a New York bank watches its own position. In what I might refer to as the "old days," the money market officer of a bank which was very far "out" in its reserve position at the Federal Reserve Bank was not considered a good money market officer. It was his task to arrange the supply of reserve funds so as to average close to the required level. Conversely, it was also his responsibility not to be short in his reserves. He had, as possibilities open to him for the adjustment of his position, the calling of brokers' loans, the selling of bills to the Federal Reserve Bank or in the discount market, or borrowing.

For a considerable number of years now, we, in the New York Federal Reserve Bank, have been measuring this flow of funds in and out of the market. The report sheet was of considerably greater use to us during the period when excess reserves were nonexistent. Those were the days when the market was nicely balanced. The movement of a small amount of funds away from New York was rather quickly followed by a somewhat tighter money situation. The movement of just a small amount of funds was usually accompanied by a movement in the call-loan rate. But now, with a couple of billions of excess reserves in New York, the market on some occasions has lost millions—sometimes $200,000,000 or $300,000,000 in a single day—and there has been no visible effect. On account of the great surplus, the loss of the funds did not cause pressure to appear in any direction.

The crux of the whole money market situation is to be found in the reserve position of the New York City banks. And the reserve position of the New York City banks is calculated, on the one hand, from the amount of reserve balances at the Federal Reserve

Bank and, on the other hand, from the reserve required to be kept. The requirement varies for various classes of banks. The so-called reserve requirement for New York City banks at the present time is that they carry 22¾ percent of demand deposits and 5 percent of time deposits. If reserve balances exceed the requirement, they have excess reserves; if reserve balances are below the requirements, they have a deficit. It is because of this relationship that the movements of funds in and out of the New York market are important. There are many transactions, of one kind or another, that effect changes in the reserve balances of the New York City banks. These transactions, either directly or indirectly, pass through the Federal Reserve Bank and, by obtaining reports from some twenty departments and divisions of the bank that handle certain types of work, the Reserve Bank is able to measure the resulting flow of funds. In times of considerable activity in the money market, it was very important to know of these movements of funds, to know of them promptly, to know to what extent the need for member bank borrowing was being built up by them, and to know what amounts of paper dealers might be going to offer to the Reserve Bank. The report sheet afforded a very convenient measurement of the flow of funds in the market. At such times, I think we had something like hourly reports, beginning at ten or eleven o'clock in the morning. With reserves as they are now, there is less interest in this sort of activity.

Without attempting to discuss all the transactions that affect the market, I should like to mention briefly a few of them. With respect to so-called commercial and agency transactions: The item of currency and coin frequently exerts a quite important influence on the money market, in fairly normal times. To the extent that the banks need additional currency from the Federal Reserve Bank, they come to the bank, obtain the currency, and have their reserves charged. There is a fairly regular pattern of currency withdrawals and deposits. There are first the distinct seasonal movements; for example, we have a low in July and August which builds up in the fall, a sharp rise just before Christmas, and then a sharp decline immediately after Christmas. All this has a considerable effect upon the reserve balances of the banks. There is also a shorter movement within the week; for example, money is drawn out on Thursday, Friday, and Saturday to meet pay rolls, tending to return during the first three days of the week, Monday, Tuesday, and Wednesday.

Of even greater consequence, in some periods, is the movement of funds between New York and other parts of the country. This is reported chiefly through two sources: transfers of money by telegraph and cash letters (check collections). On some occasions these movements of funds have reached a total of several hundred million dollars during the course of one day. Foreign account operations are sometimes very important. In recent years the operations of stabilization funds have resulted at times in a fairly large movement of funds into the market; and, on some occasions, out of the market. Another item that has been exceedingly important is gold imports. To the extent that gold imports come into this country, there is a gain to the money market in the first instance, whether this gold is to be sterilized or not. The gold import results in an increase in member-bank reserve balances, for the payment is always made either directly or indirectly to the member bank. If we are in the midst of a period of gold sterilization, such sterilization does not become effective until the Treasury has sold new securities to take funds out of the market. So much for these so-called commercial and agency transactions.

Treasury transactions, the next group to be considered, are frequently of very large volume. Within the last few months the United States Home Owners' Loan Corporation and the Reconstruction Finance Corporation have sold large new issues, and $100,000,000 and $200,000,000 came out of the New York market on single days, with no perceptible effect.

There is another set of Treasury transactions which are connected with the activity at tax periods. These come about in this way: Income tax collections are made quarterly, and the funds tend to come out of the market over a somewhat extended period. For example, during the month of March, 1939, income tax collections totaled about $500,000,000. On the sixteenth of the month something over $100,000,000 came out of the national money market. The largest sum for a single day was thus collected on the sixteenth of the quarterly month, a regular occurrence. The reason the heaviest drain appears on the sixteenth is, of course, that the taxpayers' checks have to be dispatched to the tax collectors on the fifteenth, and during the rest of that day and the ensuing night are sent to the Federal reserve bank, and in the morning of the following day are sent to the clearing house for collection. That is one sort of Treasury tax period operation which constitutes a loss of funds to the market.

There is another loss factor which is frequently present, if the Treasury is selling a new issue of securities: that is, cash payments which the banks elect to make for the new issues. Such payments come out of the market on the fifteenth of the month, the usual issue date of Government securities. The banks, of course, have the option of paying for these securities immediately in cash, or of setting up a book credit (deposit balance) to the credit of the Government and thereby retaining the funds in the money market until the Treasury needs them. When the funds are needed by the Treasury, it calls on depositors to make payment on an issue bought sometimes as much as a year previous. This is a convenient mechanism for the Treasury to employ, for the reason that funds are then taken out of the money market only at a time when they are to be put back into the money market, since the Treasury has to spend them. Thus funds are not locked up. The Treasury withdraws the funds only when it expects to put them back into the market.

At the present time the banks generally elect to pay for the new Treasury issues in cash, because of large excess reserves, but the book-credit mechanism is available.

The last item of the Treasury quarterly financing-period operations is the matter of interest payments. Interest payments on the direct debt generally occur on the fifteenth of the quarter months. They are due, of course, on the fifteenth, but the payment is not made entirely on that one day, for the reason that not all people present their coupons on the same day.

These Treasury operations have resulted on some occasions in the loss of fairly large amounts of funds to the market. In the period prior to 1930, it frequently happened that there was a large net payment into the market for a few days, and the reserve bank, in order to smooth out money rates, generally sold to the member banks participations in a short-term security which the Treasury issued to cover its temporary excess of disbursements over receipts.

The Treasury bill sale and the Treasury bill maturity are regular weekly occurrences at the present time, matching fairly well for the country as a whole. In the case of the New York market, we frequently have a Treasury bill maturity of say $90,000,000, but if the New York City market has been allotted only $50,000,000 of a new issue, a gain of $40,000,000 of funds results, because of the excess of maturities over sales of the new issue of bills.

Two other sections of our money-market report sheet—commercial and agency transactions and Treasury operations—should be mentioned. We may assume that on a given day, in the days before excess reserves existed, there was a net loss of say $50,000,000. At that time, with no excess reserves, the loss of $50,000,000 was generally accompanied by a demand for Federal Reserve Bank credit in one form or another. In part, that loss of funds was satisfied, let us assume, by the banks' selling $10,000,000 of bills to the Federal Reserve Bank, which gave them a $10,000,000 gain. The dealers, in turn, finding that they were having their loans called by the banks because the market was losing funds, needed to obtain additional funds to carry their portfolios. They would come into the Federal Reserve Bank and sell bills or Government securities under repurchase agreement; that is, in effect they would borrow

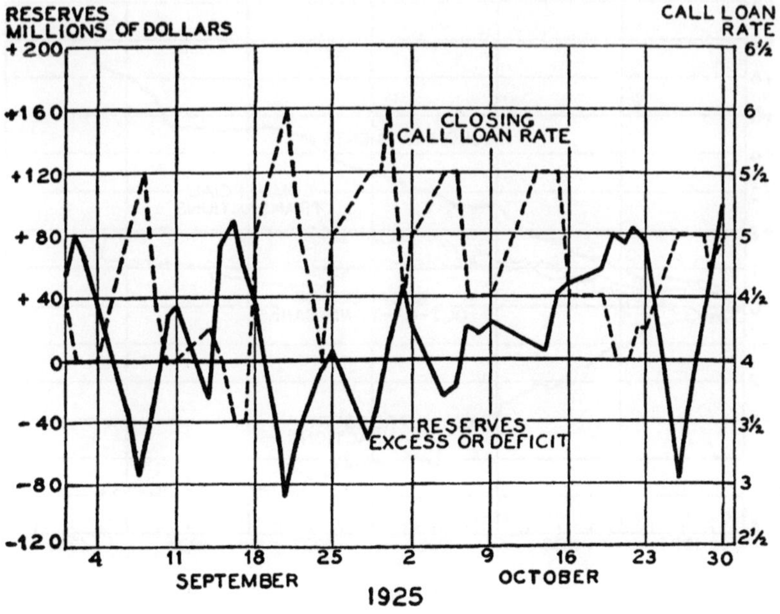

CHART II

Daily Accumulated Excess or Deficit in Reserves of 23 New York City Banks and the Closing Call Loan Rate

from the Federal Reserve Bank, supplying funds to the market thereby, also to the assumed amount of $10,000,000.

Furthermore, let us assume that the New York City banks were just about even in their reserve position and could not afford to show a net loss for the day. The net result of such a situation would be that the banks themselves would borrow something like $30,000,-000, in order to cover that part of the loss in commercial and agency and Treasury transactions not covered by the sales of bills and securities to the reserve bank. Chart II shows call money rate fluctuations in September and October, 1925, in relation to changes in the New York city banks' reserve position.

So much for the description of this work sheet, by which the

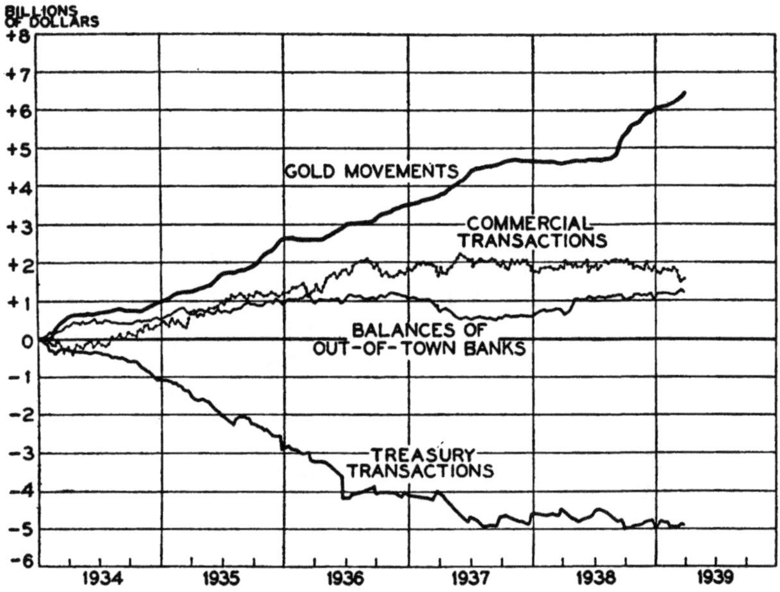

CHART III

Principal Factors Accounting for Movements of Funds In and Out of the Second Federal Reserve District (Cumulative from January 1, 1934)

Federal Reserve Bank of New York measures the flow of funds in and out of the market.

It may be interesting to trace the flow of funds during the period since January, 1934. The reason I select this date for a starting point is that it marks the devaluation of the dollar, after which the huge gold inflow began. I also wish to show the movement since that time, because in January, 1934, the New York banks held only approximately $100,000,000 of excess reserves. At the present time they have practically $2,000,000,000 of excess reserves. Query:

How did that happen? The one most significant contribution to the present situation has been the gain afforded through the gold inflow. There have been two other large gains of funds—one, a rather persistent gain in business transactions—commercial and financial funds, we call them. This flow continued approximately through the latter part of 1936 and since then has leveled off. The other movement was an inflow of interior bank balances to New York, which continued through 1936. There was some reduction in this in 1937, when reserve requirements were raised throughout the country, but a renewed flow into New York has since followed. At the present time the balances of out-of-town banks in New York are higher than they have ever been before. The offset to these gains of funds has come very largely through losses in Treasury transactions. This, in turn, is due to the fact that the Treasury has taken more out of this market through the sale of new securities for deficit financing than it has put back in the form of interest payments, relief, and expenditures for other purposes. There have been other money-market transactions as well. These, however, represent the four largest movements of funds.

George L. Bliss

The Operation of the Federal Home Loan Bank System and Its Related Agencies

IT IS my purpose to discuss, in general, the field of home mortgage finance. I will discuss the fashion in which funds are raised for that purpose, the nature and character of the financial institutions that constitute the principal sources of home mortgage credits, and, in particular, the joint efforts in recent years of both private capital and the Federal Government to eliminate the peaks and valleys in this field, to the end that there may always be an adequate supply of credit for mortgages on home properties on reasonable terms.

TWO PRINCIPAL SOURCES OF CREDIT

For a long time economists have recognized a basic principle in the classification of credits, of which the public is generally unaware. That principle was clearly in the minds of those who sponsored the legislation which established the Federal Home Loan Bank System, and was fully comprehended by the committees of Congress that conducted the hearings on the bill. That principle recognizes that demand deposit money properly belongs in the commercial banks, where it must be kept in liquid form, invested in readily marketable securities, or loaned on short-term commercial paper. It contemplates that long-term savings, or investment funds, properly belong in thrift and savings institutions and, as such, are the proper source for mortgage credits, which, by their very nature, are obviously long-term in character.

In our economic life, there is a constant clash between two groups. One of these seeks a wider recognition of this principle, and advocates a clear-cut distinction between commercial banking and the extension of commercial credits on the one hand, and savings banking, with the extension of mortgage credits, on the other hand. The other, the opposing group, either declines to recognize any such principle, or contends that it is possible to devise means by which mortgages may be furnished with the elements of liquidity now found in commercial loans and marketable securities, and hence that the distinction is unimportant.

Not only is it my belief that there is a definite and clear-cut distinction between these two forms of credit, but that the general welfare of the country will be more surely served by an increased recognition of that principle, rather than by artificial and unnatural attempts to create liquidity in mortgage investments.

As I have noted, the Federal Home Loan Bank System was established in recognition of that principle. The philosophy of its establishment was that since the Federal Reserve System had been established as the central credit agency for the commercial banks, the country would be benefited by the establishment of a credit agency created to serve the thrift and home-financing institutions. To be consistent, exponents of this school of thought might well argue that the Federal Home Loan Bank System should embrace all mortgage credits, rather than to be limited to the home mortgage field, a home mortgage being defined in the Federal Home Loan Bank Act as a first mortgage on a dwelling designed for not more than four families. However, at the time the act was passed, Congress was motivated by a particular desire to relieve credit stringency in the home mortgage field, and, for that reason, the act was confined to that field. More recently proposals have been made to enlarge the facilities of the Federal Home Loan Bank System so as to embrace all types of mortgages, and legislation in that direction is not unlikely in the future.

PRINCIPAL SOURCES OF HOME MORTGAGE CREDIT

Individuals have always been the principal source of home mortgage credit. In that category, we include not only the thrifty person who, having accumulated a sum of money, lends it on mortgage to a neighbor, but likewise trustees of estates, trustees of pension funds, fraternal organizations, endowments, and the like. The Division of Research and Statistics of the Federal Home Loan Bank Board estimates that, at the end of 1937, the total amount of home mortgages held by individuals was approximately $6,000,000,000. At that same date, home mortgages held by institutional lenders were estimated at $8,910,000,000, distributed as follows:

Savings and Loan Associations	$3,480,000,000
Mutual Savings Banks	2,700,000,000
Life Insurance Companies	1,330,000,000
Commercial Banks	1,400,000,000

Thus the total amount of home mortgages financed by private capital amounted to $14,910,000,000 at that date. The government-owned Home Owners' Loan Corporation held $2,398,000,000 in home mortgages, at the same date, constituting, for the most part, a refinancing of mortgages in distress formerly held by private lenders, both individuals and financial institutions.

For many years, savings and loan associations have constituted the largest single source of home mortgage credit in the institutional field. The first savings and loan association was organized in this country in 1831, and at the present time there are about 9,000 such institutions located throughout the country, with resources of approximately $6,000,000,000. Because their investment policy embraces home mortgages almost exclusively, they have been the most dependable source of home mortgage credit. In the period from 1920 to 1930, savings and loan associations were making about one-third of the home mortgages recorded each year. During the depression years, owing to the withdrawal from the field of other institutional lenders, the ratio of home mortgages made by savings and loan associations increased to more than one-half of the total volume. With the reëntry into the mortgage lending field of other institutional lenders during the past year or two, the proportion attributable to savings and loan associations has again dropped to approximately one-third of the total. Savings and loan associations originated the amortized home mortgage, repayable in monthly installments over a period of years.

Mutual savings banks have been the second largest source of home mortgage credits in so far as institutional lending is concerned. The first savings bank was established in 1816, and at the present time there are about 600 mutual savings banks in the country, with resources of something more than $10,000,000,000. They are to be found, however, in only seventeen of the states, and the bulk of their assets are in the six New England states, New York, and New Jersey. Such mutual savings banks as are located in the larger cities lend not only on home properties, but also upon apartment houses, office buildings, and other commercial properties. Between 50 percent and 60 percent of savings bank assets are invested in mortgages, and it is estimated that about one-half of such holdings are on home properties. In the pre-depression era, the mutual savings banks accounted for about 15 percent of the home mortgage lending, which ratio, however, steadily declined during the depression period and is now running at less than 5 percent of total volume. While some savings banks have recently adopted the monthly-payment, amortized mortgage plan developed by the savings and loan associations, the bulk of the mortgages owned by the mutual savings banks were written on the straight mortgage basis, payable at the end of from three to five years, and were frequently permitted to run overdue as demand mortgages.

Third in importance among institutional lenders are the life insurance companies. In general, life insurance companies have not been a dependable source of home mortgage credit. The very nature of the life insurance business has caused them to seek diversification of investment. That portion of their investment portfolio represented by mortgages has accordingly been distributed throughout the country, and has occasioned the companies to seek large loans for convenience in handling. Whereas the life insurance companies have been the largest single source of mortgage credit for the financing of hotels, apartment houses, office buildings, theaters, and other commercial properties, they have been interested in making or purchasing mortgages on home properties only when other investments were unavailable or were less attractive on the basis of interest rate. In the years preceding 1930, life insurance companies were accounting for approximately 9 percent of the total home mortgage financing, which ratio dropped below 2 percent in the depth of the depression, and currently is running about 9 percent again. Most mortgage loans made by life insurance companies have been on the straight mortgage basis, although during recent years an appreciable portion of their volume has been written on amortizing contracts.

An evaluation of the importance of commercial banks in the home mortgage field is difficult, because of the character of the banking business. Not infrequently the commercial bank makes a loan on an unsecured basis, and then, when difficulty is experienced in collecting the loan, requests the borrower for collateral, often taking a mortgage for that purpose. Thus a substantial portion of mortgage loans shown on the statement of a particular bank may not have originated as mortgage loans. Taking the figures at their face value, however, we find that during the period from 1925 to 1935, the commercial banks were accounting for from 10 percent to 15 percent of the total volume of home mortgage loans. It must be recognized that the purpose of the passage of the National Housing Act was to provide a method by which insured mortgages would be found attractive to commercial banks, through assurance of liquidity. The primary purpose of Title II operations of the Federal Housing Administration has been to attract the idle funds of the commercial banks into the home mortgage field, and the success of that endeavor is attested by the fact that commercial banks are currently accounting for approximately one-quarter of all home mortgage financing. It is thus interesting to note that while historically commercial banks have been the least important factor in home mortgage financing, they are, at the moment, ranking in third place, and next to the savings and loan associations in importance, in the field of institutional lending. All mortgages insured under Title II by the Federal Housing Administration must be written on a monthly-payment, amortizing contract, of the type originated by savings and loan associations.

In passing, some reference should be made to the operations of the title-and-mortgage guarantee companies which, while not of great significance in the nation-wide statistics, were a substantial factor in metropolitan New York. Such companies in New York originated approximately $3,000,000,000 of mortgages, of which it is estimated that approximately one-third were on home properties. As is well known, nearly all of such companies failed during the depression, and they are not currently a factor in the home mortgage business.

ESTABLISHMENT OF THE FEDERAL HOME LOAN BANK SYSTEM

As early as 1920, bills were introduced in Congress for the establishment of a Federal Home Loan Bank System. The early sponsors were savings and loan executives, impressed by the successful operation of the Federal Reserve System, established in 1913. The creation of the Land Bank of the State of New York, in 1915, was a further precedent. The Land Bank of the State of New York (in 1932 its name was changed to Savings and Loan Bank of the State of New York) was a central credit agency for the savings and loan associations in New York State. All of its capital stock was owned by the member institutions, and the bank demonstrated, for the first time, the feasibility of providing long-term credits for mortgage-lending institutions. At the peak of its operations, which was reached in 1932, the bank had $17,000,000 in advances outstanding to its member institutions.

With these precedents, increasing agitation for a Federal Home Loan Bank bill continued, and a resolution urging the establishment of such a system was one of the principal accomplishments of the National Conference on Home Building and Home Ownership, summoned by President Hoover in November, 1931.

As enacted, the law provides that membership in the system shall be available to savings and loan associations, insurance companies, and savings banks engaged in the making of home mortgage loans, provided the applicant institution is in sound financial condition and well managed.

The act follows rather closely the pattern of the Federal Reserve Act. Supervision of the Federal Home Loan Bank System is placed in a board of five, no more than three of whom may be members of the same political party. The board was authorized to divide the country in from eight to twelve districts, and to establish a Federal Home Loan Bank in each district. Twelve such districts have been established, but unlike the Federal Reserve districts, they follow state lines. Each of the Federal Home Loan Banks is owned by its member institutions, who are required to maintain an investment amounting to not less than one percent of the unpaid balance of their net home mortgages. The original capital of the banks, amounting to approximately $125,000,000, was furnished by the Reconstruction Finance Corporation. Each Federal Home Loan Bank is managed by a board of directors, eight of whom are elected by the member institutions and four of whom are appointed by the Federal Home Loan Bank Board. It is the policy of the board to select persons not actively engaged in the thrift and home-financing business, so as to provide direct representation of the public-interest point of view.

Among institutions eligible for membership, by far the greatest interest in the system has been displayed by the savings and loan associations. They supported the bill when it was pending in Congress, and joined the system in large numbers when it was established. The bulk of the insurance companies and savings banks have been indifferent to the system, although a few life insurance companies and savings banks, located in the smaller communities, have joined the system to insure a means of borrowing upon their mortgages in times of credit stringency. The following table classifies the membership of the Federal Home Loan Bank System as of the end of the year 1938:

Institution	*Number*	*Resources*
Savings and Loan Associations	3,903	$3,785,000,000
Insurance Companies	39	443,000,000
Savings Banks	9	201,000,000

SERVICES PROVIDED BY THE FEDERAL HOME LOAN BANKS

It is to be borne in mind that the primary purpose for which the Federal Home Loan Bank System was established was to provide a means by which member institutions of the system could secure long-term credits, collateralized by their home mortgages. The customary form of long-term credit is a ten-year advance, repayable in equal quarterly installments. Under the provision of the act, the note of the member institution securing such an advance must be collateralized by mortgages that (1) have not more than twenty years to run to maturity when presented, (2) have an unpaid principal not in excess of $20,000, (3) cover property upon which there is located a dwelling for not more than four families, and (4) are not more than six months past due. The collateral value assigned to such mortgages may not exceed 65 percent of the unpaid principal, nor more than 60 percent of the appraised value of the property, in the case of amortized mortgages written for a term of six years or longer. When the mortgage tendered as collateral is a straight mortgage, or was written on an amortizing contract of less than six years, the collateral value may not exceed 50 percent of the unpaid principal, nor 40 per cent of the appraised value of the property. Mortgages insured under Title II of the National Housing Act may be given a collateral value not in excess of 90 percent of the unpaid principal.

Advances to member institutions made by a Federal Home Loan Bank for periods of one year or less are termed "short-term advances," and may be made with or without collateral. Such advances may be made on a non-collateralized basis, when the creditor liabilities of the member institutions do not exceed 5 percent of its net assets, other than sums owed to a Federal Home Loan Bank. A Federal Home Loan Bank may, however, require short-term advances to be collateralized and, if mortgage collateral is tendered, it is subject to the same restrictions as in the case of long-term advances. Some of the Federal Home Loan Banks require periodic amortization on short-term advances, as well as on the long-term advances.

The Federal Home Loan Banks may also make both long-term and short-term advances to member institutions, with obligations of the United States Government as collateral.

The rate of interest on short-term and long-term advances to member institutions is determined by the board of directors of each Federal Home Loan Bank, subject to approval by the Federal Home Loan Bank Board. Such rates follow the money market, and the rate of interest on short-term advances has usually been lower than the rate of interest on long-term advances. When the Federal Home Loan Bank System began business in 1932, the rate of interest on advances from member institutions was 5 percent, but it has steadily declined until the prevailing range is from 3 percent to 3½ percent on long-term advances and from 1½ to 3 percent on short-term advances.

The funds with which loans are made to member institutions are derived from three principal sources. The first source, naturally, is the capital of the banks, which, as has already been stated, was furnished in part by the Reconstruction Finance Corporation, the remainder having been furnished by the required investment of member institutions in the capital stock of the banks. The investment of member institutions in the capital stock of the Federal Home Loan Banks at this time amounts to approximately $40,000,000. It might be pointed out that the act limits the amount that a member institution may borrow from a Federal Home Loan Bank to twelve times the amount of its investment in the capital stock of the bank. However, in order to qualify for a larger credit, such investment may be increased beyond the minimum requirement of one percent of net home mortgages.

The second source of funds is deposits of member institutions. Such deposits may be on a demand or a time basis, and interest is paid on deposits in accordance with rates established by the board of directors of each Federal Home Loan Bank, subject to the approval of the Federal Home Loan Bank Board. At the present time, none of the banks is paying interest on demand deposits, while on time deposits the range is from one-half of one percent to 1½ percent. Under the provisions of the act, deposits may be invested only in United States Government bonds, and in short-term advances to member institutions. They may, however, be deposited with other Federal Home Loan Banks, and in this fashion surplus funds in one part of the country are made available for Federal Home Loan Bank advances in other districts, when a need for such funds exists.

The third source of funds is the sale of Federal Home Loan Bank obligations. Up to the present time there have been sold five issues of consolidated Federal Home Loan Bank debentures, issued without collateral, as the joint and several obligations of all of the Federal Home Loan Banks. The first issue was a one-year debenture, offered in May, 1937, to yield 1½ percent. It was heavily oversubscribed, as has been the case with subsequent issues, two of which were on a one-year basis, while a three-year issue and a five-year issue have likewise been sold. The total amount of debentures issued so far is $142,700,000.

The Federal Home Loan Banks have been entirely self-sustaining. Each bank, of course, pays its own operating expenses, while the expenses of the Federal Home Loan Bank Board are borne by semiannual assessments on the twelve Federal Home Loan Banks. All of the banks have likewise paid dividends on their capital stock from the date of organization. The rate of such dividends ranges from one percent to 2 percent per annum.

In addition to the credit and deposit facilities, the Federal Home Loan Banks undertake to provide a reasonable amount of advice to member institutions, with respect to their operations. With the establishment of the Federal Home Loan Bank System, there became available, through the system, the means of compiling statistics and other data relative to the operation of thrift and home-financing institutions on a nation-wide basis. Using such material, the officers of the banks have sought to encourage member institutions to adopt modern and improved methods of conducting their operations. If the system accomplishes all that its sponsors had in mind, it will serve as a means for leveling out the peaks and valleys in the supply of funds for home mortgage credits. This means that at times when the legitimate demands for home mortgage loans in a particular community exceed the supply of funds in the hands of local lending institutions, the latter will be able to secure long-term credits with which to meet that demand, these to be repaid out of surplus funds when the tide has reversed itself. It is contemplated that in deflationary periods the banks will urge member institutions to be lenient with their credits, and that conversely the banks will exercise a reasonable curbing influence during boom periods. Time has yet to prove whether or not, in the administration of the Federal Home Loan Bank System, there will be found either the intelligence or the courage to accomplish that admittedly desirable end.

THE RELATED AGENCIES

In addition to exercising general supervision of the Federal Home Loan Bank System, embracing the twelve Federal Home Loan Banks and approximately 4,000 member institutions, the members of the Federal Home Loan Bank Board are likewise charged with the supervision of three related agencies, viz.: the Home Owners' Loan Corporation, the Federal Savings and Loan System, and the Federal Savings and Loan Insurance Corporation.

The Home Owners' Loan Corporation was the first of these agencies to be established, and came into being in 1933 with the passage of the Home Owners' Loan Act. It was created to refinance existing mortgages, when the borrower was in distress and unable to carry his existing contract. It should be explained that the Federal Home Loan Bank Act had carried a provision that, since government funds were represented in their capital, the Federal Home Loan Banks should be authorized to make direct loans to home owners "unable to obtain mortgage money from any other source." That provision proved to be unworkable. The Federal Home Loan Banks had no expense subsidy, and were without means to establish local offices to handle direct loans. Moreover, such provision was inconsistent with the basic purpose of establishing a central banking system, which was to raise its funds by selling its obligations, which in turn would have to be based on the highest grade collateral in order to secure the highest rating in the bond market. Accordingly that section was repealed, and the Home Owners' Loan Act was passed in its place. Previously, Congress had created the Federal Farm Mortgage Corporation to refinance distressed farm mortgages, and the Home Owners' Loan Act followed the same broad pattern. The members of the Federal Home Loan Bank Board were designated as the Board of Directors of the Home Owners' Loan Corporation, and for a three-year period the Home Owners' Loan Corporation was authorized to refinance existing mortgages at a 5 percent rate of interest, provided the holder of the mortgage would accept the corporation's bonds for such amount as it was willing to lend. On an average, the corporation offered bonds for approximately 90 percent of the amount of the existing first mortgage, and it frequently required that second mortgages and other liens be canceled. The new mortgage loan written by the corporation was an amortizing contract, repayable in monthly installments over a fifteen-year period. In its early operation, considerable difficulty was experienced in persuading existing mortgagees to accept the bonds of the Home Owners' Loan Corporation, and in 1934 the act was amended to provide for a guarantee by the United States Government of the principal and interest of such bonds. Within a three-year period the Home Owners' Loan Corporation made approximately 1,000,000 mortgage loans, amounting to some $3,000,000,000. Since 1936 it has been in the process of liquidation, as the act provides that all sums received by the corporation must be applied, after the payment of expenses and interest on its bonds, to the retirement of its outstanding bonds.

The Federal Savings and Loan System was created by Sections 5 and 6 of the Home Owners' Loan Act. It should be explained that for a number of years there had been some discussion, in savings and loan circles, of the desirability of providing for Federal incorporation of savings and loan associations, as a means of accomplishing uniform methods of operation and nation-wide standards of supervision in the savings and loan field. Accordingly, when some discussion occurred, relative to making the Home Owners' Loan Corporation a permanent government agency in the home mortgage field, those opposed to the permanent entry of the government into the home mortgage business urged that the Home Owners' Loan Corporation be established as an emergency agency, and that the same act authorize the incorporation of savings and loan associations under Federal charter, so as to provide a means by which local capital could be mobilized for the extension of home mortgage credits in those parts of the country in which local thrift and home-financing institutions were not already in existence. A survey, made at that time, revealed that in approximately one-half of the 3,100 counties in the United States, there were no local thrift and home financing institutions. Having provided for the incorporation of savings and loan associations under Federal charter in such localities, the act, naturally enough, contained a further provision to the effect that existing institutions that are members of the Federal Home Loan Bank System may convert to a Federal charter, if desired.

Each Federal savings and loan association is required to be a member of the Federal Home Loan Bank of the district in which it is located and, when the Federal Savings and Loan Insurance Corporation was subsequently established, that act required each Federal savings and loan association to provide likewise for the insurance of the savings of its investors. It will be noted, then, that, just as state banks and national banks have been established in the commercial banking field, so in the savings and loan field this legislation provided for the establishment of state-chartered savings and loan associations and federally chartered savings and loan associations. Up to the present time approximately 1,400 Federal savings and loan associations have been chartered, about half of them being newly organized and about half constituting conversion of state-chartered savings and loan associations. The law authorizing the chartering of Federal savings and loan associations placed the authority to issue such charters in the Federal Home Loan Bank Board, and likewise placed the responsibility for examination and supervision of such associations in the board. In practice, that supervision is decentralized through the designation of the officers of the Federal Home Loan Banks as regional agents of the board for the supervision of Federal savings and loan associations.

The Federal Savings and Loan Insurance Corporation was authorized by the provisions of Title IV of the National Housing Act, which became law in 1934. In the preceding year, Congress had created the Federal Deposit Insurance Corporation, to insure deposits in banks, and it was soon found that a similar agency was needed to insure the savings investments in savings and loan associations, if they were to accomplish a recovery in public confidence concurrently with the reëstablishment of confidence in the banking system.

This act established the Federal Savings and Loan Insurance Corporation, with an initial capital of $100,000,000 furnished by the Home Owners' Loan Corporation, and the act provided that the members of the Federal Home Loan Bank Board should serve as the Board of Trustees of the Federal Savings and Loan Insurance Corporation. The corporation insures the safety of the savings of investors and depositors in qualified savings and loan associations, up to $5,000 for each such investor or depositor. Each Federal savings and loan association must provide for such insurance of its accounts, and state-chartered savings and loan associations may qualify if, upon examination, they are found to be solvent, well managed, and engaged in sound and economical home-financing. For such insurance, each insured association must pay an annual premium of one-eighth of one percent of the total of its share capital, deposits, and creditor obligations, and the corporation may assess an additional one-eighth of one percent in any year in which its operations require it. No such additional assessments have as yet been made. In addition to the 1,400 Federal savings and loan associations, approximately 750 state-chartered savings and loan associations have qualified for insurance, so that over 2,100 savings and loan associations in the country are now provided with insurance of accounts up to the $5,000 limit. For the convenience of the insured associations, practically all of which are members of the Federal Home Loan Bank System, the Federal Savings and Loan Insurance Corporation has designated the officers of the Federal Home Loan Banks as its regional supervisory agents.

At the time that the Reconstruction Finance Corporation was investing approximately $1,000,000,000 in the capital stock of the banks of the country, in order to place them in a position to operate normally and to qualify for insurance by the Federal Deposit Insurance Corporation, Congress likewise authorized the Secretary of the Treasury to invest $50,000,000, and the Home Owners' Loan Corporation to invest $300,000,000, in the capital of state-chartered or Federally chartered savings and loan associations that were either members of the Federal Home Loan Bank System or the accounts of which were insured by the Federal Savings and Loan Insurance Corporation. Again the officers of the Federal Home Loan Banks were designated as regional agents of the Home Owners' Loan Corporation in the handling of such applications. Approximately $265,000,000 has been thus invested, the remainder being held in reserve for rehabilitation cases of extreme need.

CONCLUSION

It should be noted that the one purpose for which the Federal Home Loan Bank System and its related agencies were established was to provide machinery to the end that private capital, rather than government capital, should be the source of home mortgage credit. The purpose of all of this legislation has been to strengthen existing machinery and to add additional means so that local capital under local management shall, at all times, be adequate in amount to meet the reasonable home mortgage demands of every community in the United States.

The principal cause of distress in the home mortgage field, as it developed in the last depression, was the prevalence of the old-fashioned, short-term, straight mortgage loan, as written by all mortgage lenders other than savings and loan associations, and with no expectation of nor provision for repayment. The widespread calling of these straight mortgages at one time was a substantial cause of our economic difficulties. The Federal Home Loan Bank System was established in the belief that local thrift and home-financing institutions properly constitute the principal source of home mortgage credits; that institutions of that type should be encouraged and developed; and that a central banking system for such institutions will provide a means by which they may borrow in time of stress on the collateral of the mortgages that they own, thus enabling them to accord reasonable leniency to those mortgage borrowers who present a reasonable prospect of working their way through their difficulties. The related agencies were established to supplement the work of the system, and to round out the entire field.

Furthermore, it will be noted that the legislation that has been here reviewed, has established, in the thrift and home-financing field, a counterpart for each of the principal Federal agencies in the banking field. Just as the Federal Reserve System is a central banking agency for the banks, just as the National Bank Act provides for the establishment of banks under Federal charter, just as the Federal Deposit Insurance Corporation insures the safety of deposits up to $5,000 for each depositor in an insured state or national bank, and just as the Reconstruction Finance Corporation was created as an emergency credit agency to make commercial loans that could not be made by the banks, so the Federal Home Loan Bank System is a central credit agency for the thrift and home-financing institutions, the Federal Savings and Loan System provides a means for Federal incorporation of savings and loan associations, the Federal Savings and Loan Insurance Corporation insures the safety of each investor's savings up to $5,000 in each insured state-chartered or Federally chartered savings and loan association, and the Home Owners' Loan Corporation is an emergency credit agency for the making of mortgage loans that could not properly be made by home-financing institutions.

But there is one important difference. The four Federal banking agencies are each separate and distinct from the other. A commercial bank that deals with all four of the Federal banking agencies finds itself under the necessity of making separate reports to the several agencies, and may be subject to separate examinations by them. In the thrift and home-financing field, however, since the four agencies operate under the supervision of the Federal Home Loan Bank Board and since the Federal Home Loan Banks are the regional agents for all four agencies, the local institution that is dealing with one or more of these agencies need file but one set of reports, is subject to but one examination, and deals with but one office in the interpretation of rulings and in general supervisory matters.

Admittedly there has been so much legislation relating to banking, to mortgage financing, and to housing in recent years that it is little wonder that the public is confused and finds it difficult to understand the distinction between the several agencies. It has been my purpose to point out, however, that the legislation establishing the Federal Home Loan Bank System and its related agencies was by no means haphazard, but, on the contrary, executed step by step a well-conceived plan to integrate and increase the effectiveness with which thrift and home-financing institutions can accomplish the dual purpose of (1) encouraging the habit of thrift among persons of moderate means, and (2) of assuring an adequate supply of local credits for home-financing, to be provided by local institutions under local managements, during all phases of the economic cycle.

Benjamin Graham

Storage and Stability—A Plan for Monetizing the Commodity Surplus

A WORD at the outset with respect to the history of this proposal to monetize the commodity surplus. It was first formulated in 1921, published in 1933, and elaborated in my book, *Storage and Stability,* in 1937. I say this to indicate that the proposal is hardly an improvisation. Whatever its shortcomings, it does not suffer from lack of rather considerable thought and discussion.

I suggest the following mode of procedure: I should like first to discuss briefly the relation of my plan to the currency and credit elements. Then I shall proceed to consider in greater detail the mechanism of the plan itself, a number of its implications, its claimed advantages, and some of the criticisms that have been leveled against it.

The proposal envisages a commodity reservoir for the monetary storage of basic raw materials. The whole idea—expressed in a sentence—is to give a composite group of primary commodities the monetary status formerly enjoyed by gold under the free gold standard. Compressed into a phrase, this may be called "commodity symmetalism," into a word, "commetalism." Nevertheless, the fundamental purpose of the plan is not a monetary one. Its real objective is to deal in a direct and logical manner with the recurring problem of surplus raw materials, which has developed into so powerful a force for demoralization in our modern economy. All will agree that these surpluses, if properly handled, should be a source of strength rather than weakness. And all will agree, I think, that this paradox of want induced by plenty—of depression aggravated by abundance—is the greatest present challenge to our economic intelligence and ingenuity.

Yet since my proposal is couched in the form of a monetary measure, its salient features and objectives may be expressed in monetary terms. We have first—and, I think, least important—a new kind of money. It is currency backed by and convertible into basic raw materials, in the same way that gold certificates were backed by and convertible into gold. Whether such currency is intrinsically superior or inferior to gold is a matter of opinion and argument. If the sole measure were the practical utility of the physical backing, few would deny that a store of diversified primary commodities should constitute a better backing for paper money than the yellow metal, with its somewhat metaphysical qualities. But in any event we are not called upon to choose between the two currencies. The commodity-backed money is not intended to replace other currency—except Federal Reserve notes, to the extent these are no longer needed. It will be one more form of money added to the ten existing types. True, we have too many kinds already; but the addition of still another may be excused if thus we establish a sensible and helpful relationship between our currency structure and our national product.

The second point is that the *amount* of currency created under the plan will increase as commodities become superabundant and will decrease as a demand for them draws them out of the monetary reservoir. This is quite a different idea than that underlying the elasticity of Federal Reserve notes. But I submit that it is one better adapted to present needs—for as commodities accumulate, an increase in national purchasing power through increased currency in circulation may well prove helpful. Conversely, a contraction of the currency in the face of a speculative demand for commodities may also serve a useful end.

More important than the two preceding elements is the fact that since the plan establishes a physical equivalence between a market basket, or unit, of commodities and a paper dollar, the price of the commodity unit thereby becomes fixed *by definition.* Just as a paper dollar and twenty-three grains of gold formerly meant one and the same thing, so a paper dollar and the composite unit of commodities will mean the same, because they will also be mutually interchangeable.

What are the implications of this kind of price-fixing? First we must stress the fact that it is a *limited* stabilization of prices. No individual price is fixed, because it is only the commodity unit *as a whole* which flows into or out of the reservoir. Each component commodity is free to fluctuate in price in accordance with conditions of supply or demand, but within the framework of a fixed value for the group as a unit. Again, other price groups—finished goods, services, and so forth—are not directly stabilized by this mechanism; but we shall point out later that stability in the highly sensitive field of basic raw materials should contribute toward general price stability. We may also ask whether it is possible to have two fixed prices—one for gold and one for the commodity unit. On that point let me say that the present fixed price for gold is so artificial and so relatively meaningless, and we have such an enormous hoard of the metal available to maintain the price against advance (if such a "threat" could develop), that the relative price of gold and the commodity unit can be handled in any way we choose.

The fourth monetary aspect of my proposal is that of the store of commodities which it creates as a backing for money—corresponding to our present enormous stock or reservoir of gold. This I consider to be the central and most significant feature of the scheme. Our gold reservoir today has certain uses. It provides an extremely convenient place for gold producers to send their output, solving for them all the harsh problems of overproduction and falling prices which vex those who have other things to sell. The commodity reservoir will perform the same service for the producers of basic raw materials generally. If there is a balanced abundance in this area, and if current consumption fails to keep pace with it, it will flow into monetary storage as a backing for currency. Instead of burdening the commercial markets, depressing prices, and demoralizing general business, it will be safely impounded for future use; and instead of appearing on the economic scene in the guise of a disturbing surplus, it will be transformed into additional purchasing power in the hands of those who produced it.

Our gold reservoir is more than a mere convenience for gold miners; in theory, at least, it is an essential backing for our currency, an enormous store of national wealth, a formidable war chest, and a guarantee of strength in the international sphere. I submit that all these things which our gold stock is in theory, a true commodity reservoir should prove in actuality. Because of the overshadowing importance of this contribution of the plan to national wealth and well-being, I should like to defer discussion on this point for the moment.

Those who are keenly interested in the problems of credit control will scrutinize every proposal for its effect in this economic area. A plan for issuing currency against deposit of commodities will increase the credit-control problem to the extent that additional currency does so by adding to the credit base. But under the stimulus of our huge gold inflow, we have already developed a technique to neutralize the effect of currency expansion upon credit. There is no underlying reason, therefore, to believe that the methods of controlling credit need be any different or any less efficacious after the advent of commodity-backed currency than they are now. We should remember, also, that to a considerable extent the new currency would replace present Federal Reserve notes.

In one important respect, however, the commodity-reservoir plan should simplify the problems of credit control. These are accentuated by speculative booms in commodities and collapses in the general price level. Both of these harmful developments would be largely obviated by the reservoir mechanism. For this would keep the prices of raw materials on a level by sending out commodities when speculation or other causes tended to advance prices, and by taking them in (as complete units) when offerings would otherwise break the market.

I shall now describe in greater detail how this relatively simple idea of commodity-backed currency can be made operative. We would start by setting up the commodity unit. This should consist of all the important storable raw materials dealt in on commodity exchanges. The quantity of each in the unit should be proportionate to relative production or consumption (whichever is higher) during a base period—which, in my calculations, has been taken as the decade 1921–30. At the present time there are twenty-three commodities eligible for inclusion in the unit, as follows:

Foods: Wheat, barley, cocoa, coffee, corn, cottonseed oil, oats, rye, and sugar;

Fibers: Cotton, silk, wool;

Metals: Copper, lead, tin, zinc;

Other commodities: Cottonseed meal, flaxseed, hides, petroleum, rubber, tallow, tobacco.

These twenty-three commodities had an average annual value of just about $10,000,000,000 during the years 1921–30, and they represented about half of the total output and net imports of raw materials during this period. If iron, coal, and lumber were included—and they could readily be made eligible—the total value of the component commodities would rise to $13,500,000,000, or about two-thirds of the raw-materials aggregate. Evidently, such a group would be sufficiently comprehensive to represent a large proportion of our national economy.

The choice of the price level is one calling for our best judgment, nor is any particular level an essential part of my plan. On the whole, I think there are good reasons for choosing the average price level of 1921–30, which is about 6 percent lower than the 1926 figure, often taken as "normal" in the past. The composition of the one-dollar unit may be found very simply by dividing the annual quantities of each commodity by an appropriate number. To establish the 1921–30 level, for instance, the divisor would be about $10,000,000,000. On this basis 1,000 one-dollar units would be found to include some 84 bushels of wheat, 268 bushels of corn, 1,300 pounds of sugar, and so on, for the twenty-three items.

Having established the unit, its equivalence to the paper dollar would be maintained very simply. Anyone could present commodity units to the Treasury and get paper dollars, or present paper dollars and get units. Actually the "coinage" and the redemption of the units would come about through the activities of specialists, or arbitrageurs, operating on the various commodity exchanges. Whenever the prices of the different items showed the market value of the unit to be slightly less than a dollar, the arbitrageurs would accumulate units by purchase on the exchanges, and then present them (i.e., the warehouse receipts) for coinage into money. Conversely, whenever the value of the commodities rose slightly above the monetary equivalent, the specialists would present dollars for conversion, or redemption into commodities, and would sell these on the several exchanges. As an obvious result of this mechanism, the price level of the commodities in the units as a whole could never fall more than a small amount below the standard level, since then it would be profitable for anyone to buy the commodities and "coin" them. The converse would be true, as long as there were any commodity units in monetary storage. The analogy between this mechanism and the maintenance of the dollar-sterling rate under the gold standard is too obvious to need elaboration.

The commodity unit could be revised, say every ten years, to reflect changes in the relative position of the various commodities. In my book, *Storage and Stability,* I explain in detail the technique of such revisions, of the addition of new components, and also of dropping an individual commodity if its price advances excessively. More important in practice than the latter point is the provision for replacing the physical or spot commodities by contracts in futures (together with cash to take them up), whenever this can be done at a saving. The great advantage of this arrangement is that it will permit the country to draw upon the stock of an individual commodity whenever there is a temporary shortage, owing to drought or other causes. Such conditions of temporary scarcity are invariably marked by much higher prices for the spot commodity than for the future deliveries. (During 1937, for instance, this spread was as high as 58 percent for corn, and 45 percent for barley.) By the replacement device, the reservoir can be used to ease individual shortages, on terms which will help defray the cost of storage.

These costs are, of course, an important element on the debit side of the plan. My calculations lead to the conclusion—partly tentative—that storage of commodity units on a comprehensive and economical scale (including, e. g., storage of corn on the farm) should be possible at not more than a cost of 3 percent annually. Assuming an average holding of one-half year's supply—and our policy could be directed to such a figure, if we wished—the annual expense would amount to about $150,000,000. This is in itself neither a small nor a large sum. If for this amount we can turn surplus from a source of demoralization and deep depression into a bulwark of national strength and prosperity, it would seem a negligible price to pay for the solution of the paradox of want amid plenty. Our water reservoir system is undoubtedly costing us much more than $150,000,000 a year; valuable as it is, it cannot compare in possible benefits with a really effective reservoir of our basic raw materials.

It is time to dilate a little upon these benefits. Negatively, the mere diversion of surplus to a safe place, instead of letting it ruin the price structure and business confidence, would be of inestimable value—comparable, at least, to the flood-control function of our water reservoirs. But positively, the values are even more imposing. Let me mention four separate uses for the commodity store: in war, in drought, as a social security reserve, and—most important of all—as the physical lever to raise the national standard of living. Those who lived through the last World War remember the heatless Sundays, the meatless Mondays, the rationing of sugar and flour, and so forth. Practically every one of the basic commodities in our unit would become relatively scarce in war time. Hence the commodity reservoir might well make the difference between comfort and privation—if not between victory and defeat. Under modern conditions it should prove a far more formidable war chest than our gold hoard; and, as such, it might be expected to daunt a potential aggressor as effectively as any armament.

In the droughts of 1934 and 1936, the reservoir would readily have alleviated shortages which required large imports of food and sharply raised the price of meat. I suggest also, that since we have instituted an old-age pension system, through which those retiring from work are to be supported, what more practical reserve against this accruing national liability could we establish than a supply of commodity units? For these comprise, directly or indirectly, most of the things our pensioners will consume. The proposed $47,000,000,000 reserve, consisting entirely of our own debt, has properly been viewed with skepticism bordering on ridicule. A partial reserve in the form of several billions of commodity units—represented by commodity currency held in the fund—would constitute at once a sound provision for the future needs of the aged and a valuable use for our surplus commodities.

But this idea leads immediately to a better, because a more comprehensive one. Obviously the true destiny of accumulated plenty is to supply greater sustenance and ampler comfort for the entire nation. It should not be a serious challenge to our social and economic statesmanship to find means—*at our leisure and under no stress of sudden depression*—to bring the stored abundance into consumption, by directing the money issued against it into the hands of the many poorer citizens who are only too ready to spend and consume.

Perhaps I can throw some further light on this central aspect of my proposal by considering two sorts of objections which have been advanced against it. One set of critics, leaning to the conservative side, have visions of America overwhelmed beneath a veritable flood of commodities. Thinking in commercial terms, they see business menaced by this abundance, as it was in 1931–32. Other critics, who are social rather than business-minded, are hostile to the idea of a reservoir because they see no reason why all production—however large—should not *immediately* be directed to fill the unlimited potential demands of our population. But in reality my plan is intended to meet the demands of one group and to allay the fears of the other. For, on the one hand, the commodity reservoir is an engineering device by which we can manage an unlimited supply without demoralizing our business structure. It shunts the excess from the commercial markets, where it does untold harm, to an entirely non-commercial resting place, where it is safely impounded and mobilized for later use when we are ready for it.

On the other hand, those who think that purchasing power should be so distributed that effective demand will always equal supply are imposing unnecessarily difficult conditions on the world of tomorrow. All reservoirs—whether of water in a local tank, or of sugar in the human body, or even of goods in a warehouse—are intended to facilitate the adjustment of supply to demand so as to permit more even and more liberal consumption. Our Catskill reservoir does not deprive New Yorkers of water which they otherwise could consume. On the contrary, it is only because of these abundant resources in storage that we can afford to be as liberal and as care-free as we are with the precious fluid. If this point were thought through, I am sure all would realize that the commodity reservoir can mean only abundance and not deprivation.

I shall now speak as briefly as possible of a number of the aspects of my proposal which are collateral to the broad objectives, and about which there are no doubt unspoken questions. First, what bearing has this proposal upon the great enigma of the business cycle and the related but not identical problem of unemployment? In my view, business cycles are aggravated, rather than initiated, by changes in the commodity price level which follow on increasing demand or a condition of oversupply. Up swings or down swings of business are more likely to get their start from credit conditions, or the state of business inventories, or changes in demand for durable goods induced, perhaps, by psychological reasons. But the significant point is that business booms do not often go very far without speculation in commodities, and severe depressions are invariably marked by a collapse in the commodity price level. A plan for preventing both wide advances and wide declines in the price level cannot fail, therefore, to exercise a restraining influence of the first order upon the amplitude of our trade cycles. Complete suppression of cyclical change may be as undesirable as it is impossible—so Dr. Goldenweiser thinks, for example—but surely none will deny that we would be better off with much milder fluctuations than we have been living through of late. This, I submit, should be a prime benefit obtainable from the commodity reservoir system.

To the extent that the unemployment problem is cyclical, it should be greatly ameliorated by the damping of the swing of business. To the extent that it is technological and secular, I think that we shall be better equipped to deal with it effectively when we are free to produce in balanced abundance. Certainly the larger production made possible by the "reservoir market" should provide many more jobs.

The reservoir plan is largely a measure for farm relief, since two-thirds to three-quarters in value of the stored commodities will be produced on farms. To permit the farmer to produce freely, provided acreage is properly apportioned among the several crops, and to provide an unlimited market at a fair price for this balanced output, should clearly provide a better solution to the agricultural problem than our highly criticized recent policies of curtailment, bonuses, dumping abroad, and even destruction. Yet I have stressed the word "balanced" to bring home the fact that my plan cannot solve the separate riddle of our cotton and wheat acreage, which has become far greater in relation to other crops than world conditions will now justify. Clearly some means must be found of a *particular character* to bring cotton and wheat production in line with present-day conditions. The reservoir plan offers a twofold help in this direction. First, to the extent that it absorbs cotton and wheat along with other commodities, it relieves the pressure of oversupply. More important, it will permit us to approach the problem of cotton and wheat as a specialized affair—and not as part of a general policy of curtailment—which is indefensible, nor of expansion—which is probably impracticable for these two staples. Once we have planned for coördinated expansion of output in general, we can deal realistically with unbalance in particular fields.

Some further discussion of the price stabilization feature of the plan may be called for. There has been a great clamor for price stability, but the whole idea has also been severely criticized as impracticable and unsound. The Federal Reserve Board, for example, has recently stated that it lacks the power to stabilize prices, that price stability may coexist with unsound business conditions, and that stability of a group price means penalizing certain individual prices because others rise. In a sense, we are not concerned with the general controversy over price stabilization, because we are suggesting solely a physical *definition* of a paper dollar as *meaning* a certain market basket of commodities. It is difficult to see how such a definition can be objected to on any logical grounds, or why it is not at least as sensible to say that a dollar shall mean a commodity unit as that it shall mean fifteen grams of gold.

The criticism that a rise in one item entails a decline in others will not stand analysis, because the *relative* value of the individual commodities in the group would be the same whether the reservoir was in operation or not. Stability for raw materials would not be incompatible with the desideratum of slowly declining secular prices for finished goods, based on improved technology. In the past two hundred years, during which our amazing industrial progress has taken place, the prices of raw materials have fluctuated widely, but have shown no secular trend. Our plan would thus mean no break with past tendencies, except in so far as it suppresses wild fluctuations, which assuredly have not contributed to prosperity or progress.

As for the relation between a stabilized price level for raw materials and that of other price groups, it should be evident that these other prices would likewise tend to be stabilized to a considerable degree. For it is the wide changes in basic commodities which are mainly responsible for important price movements in other fields.

How would the institution of a commodity-backed currency affect foreign exchange and foreign trade? Since exchange rates are now largely a matter of control and agreement, the question is scarcely relevant to modern conditions. I am convinced that we can use both our gold stock and the new commodity reservoir as strong balance wheels to hold world prices for basic commodities fairly level. But, in any event, we have several feasible alternatives. Assuming, as some fear, that a drop in world prices would direct huge quantities of commodities to our shores, we could readily take them in as additional commodity units, sending out some of our gold in exchange. In the long run that should prove a very profitable exchange. If we should prefer not to take in any more commodities, we could raise our tariffs, which already penalize foreign sellers twenty-three cents on each dollar unit. Or we could let foreign exchange rates fluctuate, while we maintained a stable price level at home.

The commodity-unit mechanism should supply a simple way of dealing with the vexing problem of balances due from abroad. By accepting commodity units, we could settle these balances, add to our national wealth, and avoid the bogey of foreign goods flooding domestic markets.

I should like to close on this note of adding to our national wealth. No one doubts for a moment that our huge national resources underground are the source and the guarantee of our future prosperity. Yet we have grown accustomed to view the appearance of these same resources *above ground* with the utmost apprehension, as harbingers of depression and disaster. So in our dealings with foreign countries we would much rather accept doubtful I.O.U.s or ambiguous gold and silver than goods which could add to our national well-being. Clearly we need an arrangement—an engineering device, if you will—which can make essential raw materials above ground as harmless and as potentially valuable as our other natural resources underground. This is the aim of the monetary-reservoir plan. The simple interchangeability of paper money and a commodity composite should solve at one time the problem of providing a sound and adequate currency and the graver problem of an economic system disabled by its own productivity.

William Adams Brown, Jr.

The Probable Future of Gold

IN RECENT months the spectacle of a large and persistent transfer of gold to the United States, continued over many years and on a scale never before witnessed, has revived the discussion of the maldistribution of gold of the early 1930's and has added quite a new note of urgency to that discussion. Instead of a dispassionate economic argument about the economic effects of "maldistribution" in League of Nations Reports and other documents, a popular question has arisen concerning the future usefulness of gold as a money material. What is being asked today is "Has Gold a Future?" All answers to such a question in a world like ours must be largely speculative, but in spite of this I have been asked to try my hand at it. I shall do so with a full realization that the speculative element in my answer may be raised to the nth power by the outbreak of war, which will force upon us a fresh consideration of this, as of almost every other economic problem.

I do not, at present, think that a future demonetization of gold which will simply leave America holding the bag, as is often suggested, is probable. I think we are on, and shall continue to use, a form of international managed gold bullion standard. This does not mean that I am not in accord on many points with those who are convinced that gold has no future. For example, I am sure that most economists would hold

1. That the future of gold, if any, will be different from its past.
2. That too much gold in a banking system is a curse.
3. That the United States has too much gold in its banking system and therefore is subject to this curse, and, as a corollary, that we

have given a large amount of goods and services for something that we do not want.

4. That any attempt at a wholesale redistribution of gold is a remedy worse than the disease (I *hope* that most economists would agree on this after our experiences with redistribution after 1927).

Let me begin with the statement that the future of gold will be different from its past. Many people may agree on this statement, and yet if they really disagree on what the past of gold has been there is no meeting of minds. On this point I think that there is rather a wide-spread tendency to accept too uncritically a simple textbook explanation of the past of gold based on the Ricardian gold-flow analysis. I think that this analysis gives a very unrealistic and historically inaccurate account of the process by which gold distribution was carried out internationally before the war, and consequently I am not disheartened by finding that this present world of ours is a very inhospitable soil in which to cultivate a price-specie-flow plant. I think it is a non-sequitur to say that the automatic corrective forces of the international gold standard no longer work out, and therefore the usefulness of gold as a monetary standard is ended. We are searching for alternatives to a system that gave stability and we should reject no tools, including gold, which will help us to find them.

The attention of writers on the pre-war gold standard has long been concentrated upon the delicate and indeed wonderful mechanism by which the final balance of a world economic system already fundamentally in equilibrium (I almost said a moving equilibrium but I realize that such phrases are fighting words among theorists) was achieved, and some of them have neglected the deeper relationships which existed between gold movements and the credit operations involved in the financing of international trade and in long-term international lending.

Before the war London was the center for the distribution of most of the world's newly produced gold and for the world's trade in gold. This distribution was intimately bound up with the great credit operations of London as the world's financial center. Gold movements, therefore, were responsive both to the requirements of short run exchange stability and to the needs of the world's banking and currency systems. The long-run distribution of gold was so related to long-term international lending that the rapidly developing countries were in the main enabled to satisfy their expanding credit requirements without frequent and violent checks due to inadequate gold reserves and without upsetting the conditions required for maintaining exchange stability. In this system I believe, in full agreement with my research colleague Mr. C. J. Smit, that credit was the most important equilibrating factor, and I also believe that long-run exchange stability was mainly due to the necessity which smaller nations were under to adjust their economies to conditions existing in the larger countries, especially England; to the existence of world prices for staples as common elements in most price systems; and to the presence of a time-bridging financial mechanism, of which gold movements were a part, capable of tiding over seasonal and cyclical strains and sufficiently flexible to allow for the factor of unequal rates of economic growth in various countries.

In such a system the influence of gold movements on prices, working first through bank reserves and then through increasing the means of payment in the gold-receiving country and the reverse in the gold-losing countries, may have been at times an operative mechanism, but I believe that the forces regularly and continuously at work bringing price levels into a sufficiently harmonious relationship to permit exchange stability were far more powerful, far more reliable, and far more direct than this.

We shall, I believe, never secure a durable system of stable exchange rates (I am dodging, I am well aware, a large issue about whether we do want this or not) by chasing the rainbow of an oversimplified specie-flow mechanism such as that frequently attributed to the pre-war international gold standard system. What is, I think, more important is that we shall never get it by returning to what we actually had before the war. For the essentials of what was in effect a world-wide sterling exchange standard will not be recreated.

Nor shall we ever return to the type of international distribution which we had from 1925 to 1931. The most important difference (there were many differences) between the system of 1925 to 1931 and the pre-war system as far as gold distribution is concerned was that the relative importance of the London bullion market in the world distribution of gold was much reduced. This was chiefly due to the fact that gold distribution through London no longer stood in its pre-war relation to British long-term lending. London's "gold income" from South Africa was no longer an additional source of strength for sterling, added to a strong underlying balance of payments position and potentially available at all times to strengthen the Bank of England reserve by appropriate modification of the export of capital, but it was an offset against an underlying weakness. From 1925 to the middle of 1928, for example, the Bank of England was protected from strong if intermittent demand for gold from Germany by the policy of the Reichsbank. The main burden of supplying gold to South American countries in connection with currency reforms and as a result of trade balances was taken from the London market and transferred to New York as a result of American loans. The sudden French demand for gold in 1927 was diverted to the United States by the inter-central bank arrangements of that year. The greatest single change in the economic significance of the flow of England's gold income through the London bullion market after 1925, as compared to pre-war days, was that it no longer gave adequate assurance that British international credit operations could be carried out without apprehension concerning their effect on the gold standard in England.

The protection of the gold standard in England was confided in large measure to the American capital market, and the pound sterling was exposed to danger whenever America was under-lending.

The gradual withdrawal of the support given to the whole system of stable exchange rates by American lending began toward the end of 1928 and brought to the surface all the latent differences between the flow of gold through the London bullion market after 1925 and that of pre-war days. In 1929 the recurrence of the pre-war phenomenon that in times of crisis gold flows from debtor to creditor countries showed that the price which England had to pay for being relieved of the burdens of gold distribution in part was that she was also deprived of the power of attracting gold when the time came that she needed that power.

It is obvious that we shall not return to the type of international gold distribution which we had from 1925 to 1931. Large-scale American foreign lending will not be used for long periods and cannot be used permanently to support a fundamentally artificial system of exchange rates in a fundamentally unbalanced world economy.

There was a third and entirely different system of international gold distribution during the years 1919 to 1924. This was a system which some economists seem to think has now been, or is likely soon to be, substituted for the pre-war method as rigid orthodox theory conceives it to have been. My estimate of the probable future of gold is different from the estimate of those who think that the usefulness of gold in monetary systems has been destroyed by the impossibility of returning to a simple price-specie-flow mechanism, and by our actually having returned to a situation like that of 1919 to 1924; because I take the view that we never did depend basically for the successful use of gold as a part of a world monetary mechanism upon the price-specie-flow mechanism, and that we have not now returned, and are not likely soon to return, to the 1919–1924 system of gold distribution. It is therefore important to look at the situation which prevailed from 1919 to 1924 when New York was in a true sense *a residual buyer of gold.*

After September, 1919, the magnitude of the stream of gold reaching America was a function of:

1. The volume of newly produced South African gold reaching London and having a license for export.
2. The division of this stream of gold between the consumer demand which was effective in the London bullion market and the monetary demand represented by the standing offer of the United States Treasury to buy all gold offered to it at a fixed price.
3. The amount of special shipments sent to America by governments and central banks.

The basic price in the London market was the New York shipping parity. This was arrived at by taking the American bid of $20.67 per fine ounce, translating it into shillings at the current rate of exchange and deducting the cost of shipment to New York. Whatever affected the sterling dollar exchange affected the price of gold in London, which rose and fell with the dollar. The amount of gold which went to America at this price was what was left over after true consumer demand from India and the arts was satisfied.

I do not think that we have essentially returned to this system and I do not think that, in spite of appearances to the contrary, we are now truly a residual buyer of gold, and therefore I do not look forward in the *reasonably predictable* future to demonetization of gold, unless our whole political and social system is completely altered, as the result of a suicidal world war, for example.

Now of course if we try to make guesses about the long future, anything may happen, including the demonetization of gold in the manner suggested by some economists, some journalists, and, if I may say so, by the New Yorker. On the other hand it is also conceivable that a world-wide inflation caused by the armament race and the convulsions which may follow some future attempt to revert to peacetime economies may result in some sort of general effort to impose a limit on the powers of banking systems to create means of payment, by the effective use of metallic reserves as limiting funds again. (Of course in such a situation 100 percent money might enter into a world-wide glory.) It is further conceivable that the necessary scarcity of gold enabling it to perform such a function might not be present. I read, for example, in the New York *Herald Tribune* that

> If one should throw a handful of small blocks of wood and stone into water the wood floats and the stone sinks. A separation of the wood and the stone has been thus affected, because the wood is lighter than the water and the stone heavier. Most stones have a specific gravity of between 2.3 and 2.73. Metals have much higher specific gravities, iron 7.8, copper 8.9, lead 11.0, mercury 13.5, gold 19.0, and platinum 21.5 [we have an advantage over Russia there]. If a liquid of a specific gravity of three is available and a mixture of pieces of metal and pieces of stone is thrown into it the stone floats and the metal sinks.

This is known as the sink-or-float method and it has an ominous sound. For such a heavy liquid has been found, and I read further:

> The sink-or-float process increases 600% the capacity of a mill for dressing some common ores, or conversely a given amount of metal can be obtained with a plant one sixth the size formerly required. . . . The process will have a profound effect on gold mining. Deposits which cannot now be worked at a profit because of the large amount of material that must be treated to extract its gold content will be transformed into rich [*sic*] sources of gold. This means a pending great increase in the world's supply of gold. This is likely to be more potent in producing far reaching economic effects than all past government edicts in raising the price of gold.

Though it is only indirectly germane to my subject I can hardly forebear, on Adolf Hitler's birthday, from reading further as follows:

The sink-or-float process will change the whole aspect of the natural resources map of the world, producing new relations between the have and have not nations with probably resulting changes in the political aspects.

I can only say that I hope this sink-or-float process will be easier on the nerves than the one we are having now.

It is also conceivable that we may be destined to see the universal adoption of planned economies and the exchange control that goes with it, though I have always thought that exchange control schemes flourish best as parasites on the living body of a free exchange system.

But I think it is rather futile to speculate upon the very long future. What I think we are most likely to see in the near future is a continuous attempt to develop a workable managed international gold bullion standard on the present foundations *with a minimum of gold redistribution.* Proposals for large-scale gold redistribution remind me of a story which Professor Condliffe told the other day. I hope he didn't tell it here. It was, I am sorry to say, about an Irishman. This Irishman had returned home after a visit to America. "The Americans are a wonderful inventive people," he told his friend. "In Chicago they have a wonderful great machine and they put the cows into one end of this machine and they come out as beefsteaks and leather shoes and bottles of condensed milk." "Well," said his friend, "what do they do if they get too much condensed milk and too little meat and shoes?" "Why," he said, "they are a wonderful inventive people. They have a lever in the middle of the machine which they pull which changes all the proportions just the way they want them." "That's wonderful," said his friend, "but what do they do if they get too much of everything?" "Why, that's the most wonderful thing of all. They have a great big lever at one end which they pull and all the cows walk out again where they came in." Well I believe very strongly that in economics two wrongs don't make a right. We can't pull that reverse lever. Our golden cow won't walk out again entirely the same creature from the machine we have put her through in the last twenty years.

Now if it is probable that we shall continue to try to develop a workable system on present foundations, it is important to be clear as to what these foundations are and in what way they differ from the situation which prevailed from 1919 to 1924.

We at present have a very peculiar type of managed international gold bullion standard. Two questions concerning this system are practical politics at the present moment:

1. Is there anything in the *nature* of its *mechanism* which makes the United States a residual buyer of gold, forced to stand passively by while others continually send gold to us in exchange for our goods, and completely impotent to take any initiatives to reverse this inflow.
2. Is there anything in the nature of the forces now bringing gold to our shores which makes it likely that *under present circumstances* the use of this mechanism will result in all the rest of the world's monetary gold coming to us.

Of course if the answer is yes to these questions, the thesis of those who say that gold, as money, has no future is sustained.

Let us now look at the present practices of the London bullion market with the aid of the Monetary Survey of the League of Nations.

At the present time the English "authorities maintain no fixed price for gold in the United Kingdom. The London gold market is a free gold market where quotations fluctuate from day to day under the influence of demand and supply, even though the Exchange Equalization Account *being the largest single buyer and seller of gold in London* plays an important part in controlling the market. There is, however, one important standard to which the price of gold in London has to adjust itself, namely the buying price of the United States Treasury (*$35 per fine ounce less the handling charge of 1/4%*)." That handling charge is important, for its presence determines the wide spread between the gold export and gold import points in our streamlined international gold bullion standard. "The American buying price expressed in terms of sterling at the current exchange rate, *less* the handling charge and *less* the cost of shipment from London to New York determines the so-called *shipping parity*." This is our old friend of 1919 to 1924 again. "That is the price at which a shipment of gold from London to New York yields neither profit nor loss. This parity is of course by no means fixed, but varies with the dollar rate on London. If the actual market price of gold in London falls below the shipping parity, a *discount* appears making shipments to New York profitable. If on the other hand the price is above the shipping parity, gold is said to be at a premium, which if it rises sufficiently high tends to induce shipments from New York to London. . . . The *premium* above shipping parity, unlike the discount, does not call private arbitrage into play, as the American Treasury sells gold only to central banks and Treasuries of countries adhering to the Tripartite Monetary Agreement of the autumn of 1936" (Belgium, France, the Netherlands, Switzerland and the United Kingdom). "Theoretically therefore no limit is set to the rise of the premium apart from the action taken by the authorities. It has been calculated that gold shipments from New York to London would become profitable [if private arbitrage were permitted] when the premium reached one shilling and tenpence." Some gold did move from New York to London at about this price in 1937.

Now all this means a little more than it seems to. It means that:

1. For every rate of exchange between New York and London there is established a range within which the price of gold can fluctuate in London without inducing either a private gold arbitrage shipment from London to New York or creating a situation in which a private gold arbitrage shipment from New York to London would be profitable if permitted. The general terms of

the tripartite monetary agreement indicate that the American authorities will (and there is evidence that in 1937 they did) take the place of gold arbitrageurs for export under these circumstances. This range is about one shilling tenpence—a very wide range indeed when one considers that fluctuations in the price of gold in London before the war of one and one half pence was sufficient to distribute newly produced gold to all the countries of the world.

2. For every price of gold established in the London market there is a corresponding range, amounting to seven or eight cents per pound, within which the sterling dollar rate may fluctuate without opening up opportunities for gold arbitrageurs, or official bodies performing the functions of gold arbitrageurs, to make gold shipments to or from New York.

Let us now assume that it is the policy of the British and American authorities to confine the fluctuations in the sterling dollar rate within a range of seven or eight cents around a given rate. This is certainly in accordance with the experience of the three years preceding the Czecho-Slovak crisis last September. Let us further assume that the policy of the French authorities is to keep the sterling franc rate stable and that in order to do this the French stabilization fund stands ready to buy gold at a certain price in francs and to sell gold at a slightly higher price in francs. Then for every sterling-franc rate there is established a *Paris shipping parity* in the London bullion market, and a French offering price for gold in London. This is in accordance with experience and the tripartite monetary agreement. The range between these two would naturally be and is much narrower than the range between the *New York shipping parity* and the New York offering price for gold, corresponding to any given dollar-sterling rate. Provided that the French buying and selling prices for gold in London thus established fall within this latter range, one of the main features of the existing mechanism is established. I can make this clear by stating two cases not at variance with past experience.

First: if the dollar-sterling rate is being held stable and the *Paris shipping parity in London*—that is the price at which it is just profitable to buy gold in London for shipment to France—is just above the New York shipping parity, then the franc may rise through a considerable range without causing any shipment of gold from New York to London or to France. It may rise through a range wide enough to increase the French bid for gold in London by about one shilling and tenpence. But though this may not move gold from New York, the French bid may become the highest in London and move newly produced gold on offer in London to France or it may reach a point where the British Equalization Account will sell and English gold will move to France. If now, having risen by this much, the franc begins to fall in London, it may fall through a somewhat larger range, that is, until the French offer to *sell* gold in London reaches the New York shipping parity, before French gold on offer in London will begin to move to New York. But on the way down, the French bid for gold may cease to be an effective competitor for newly produced gold and the French offering price may fall below the bids of others in the market, for example, the Belgian bid or the bid of the British Exchange Equalization Account.

All this assumes the dollar-sterling rate stable. My second example is when the franc-sterling rate is assumed to be stable (resulting in a fixed French demand price for gold in London) and the sterling-dollar rate is moving. Suppose, to start with, that the fixed French bid for gold is just under the point at which it would be profitable to ship gold from New York for sale in London for French account. Then the sterling-dollar rate might fall—that is, the dollar appreciate in London—by as much as seven or eight cents to the pound before the New York shipping parity would be high enough, first to compete with the French bid, and then to make it profitable to buy gold in France for shipment to New York. It might fall again by a similar amount before it became profitable to ship gold from New York to France.

I give these two examples to establish the fact that a considerable amount of fluctuation in the sterling-dollar rate and in the sterling-franc rate and in the London price of gold *is consistent with* the maintenance of a policy by all hands to keep exchanges stable *within a given range*. This range may be considerably narrowed by the Exchange Equalization funds of England, France, and the United States by mutual purchases and sales of gold that counteract the prevailing tendencies in the exchange market.

Now it may be (and in practice the great gold flow to America is the result of the fact that it often has been) the case that there is a tendency for one or another of the exchanges involved to move out of this general range altogether, and I want to take the two following cases to illustrate what happens then.

First let us assume that the French franc is very weak in both sterling and dollars and that the sterling-dollar rate is stable. If the French authorities are determined to resist this weakness and maintain the sterling-franc rate stable (by hypothesis of a stable sterling-dollar rate this means a stable dollar-franc rate also), then they must get pounds (and dollars) to sell against the market offer of francs. If they maintain their offer to sell gold at a fixed price in francs, the declining value of francs against sterling means that gold is being offered cheaply for French account in London. If there are no bids for gold in the London market higher than the New York shipping parity, French gold will be bought for shipment to New York. If the British fund supports the franc by buying francs in the market, it will have to decide whether to keep an open position in francs and run an exchange risk in doing so, or convert the francs into gold in Paris. If it converts, the French fund will be depleted. This choice will confront the American fund also if it too supports the franc. In the ordinary routine such conversions are instantly made as we learn from Mr. Morgenthau's letter to Senator Wagner or by reading *Fortune*. But if the French franc's weakness is very great, and not offset by English or American lending, etc., then the two funds will be faced with the problem of whether to drain out all the gold in the French fund, or take large open positions in francs, or permit the French bid to become again competitive in the London market for gold by having the French fund raise its buying price for gold in francs, thus starting the mechanism going again on a new basis. They have taken the last alternative on several occasions. In our managed international gold bullion standard that is what French devaluation means.

The second example is the case where the dollar is so strong in sterling and other currencies in this system that the New York shipping parity price rises to a point where it is the highest bid of all in the London gold market, and all gold offered, either newly produced, or offered by the funds to support their currencies, goes to New York. We read in Mr. Morgenthau's letter and in *Fortune* that a system is in operation whereby the British Equalization Fund quotes to the American fund a price for gold in shillings at the beginning of every day. This price may be a little lower than the shipping parity price to New York corresponding to the sterling-dollar rate below which the two funds do not wish sterling to fall *on that day*—at any rate it bears a close relationship to it. The example given in *Fortune* assumes the British fund to have been supporting sterling at $4.80. It quotes a price of 145 shillings per ounce to the American fund. Later in the day sterling falls to $4.78, and the American fund buys sterling at that price and converts this sterling into gold at 145 shillings per ounce at the close of the day at a small profit. But this does not mean that the New York shipping parity price of gold may not have risen sufficiently high with the appreciation of the dollar to bring new gold, French gold and other gold to America. If the weakness of sterling is very fundamental and pronounced, the same problem which, in the other example, confronted the English and American funds with regard to accumulating an open position in francs or draining the French fund may now confront the American fund. Shall it drain the British fund of gold, take an open position in sterling or agree to an increase in the sterling price at which the British fund will buy gold? The last alternative means that the dollar may appreciate still further before the American fund can profitably buy sterling and convert it into gold. Such an appreciation may mean that the dollar has risen completely out of the previously contemplated range of stabilization and that a readjustment throughout the system has to take place. Such a readjustment may be orderly if it is done by agreement, and a range may be found within which the mechanism *can* work as a stabilization mechanism. Unless there is something in the laws of nature that says the dollar must *forever* rise in value in terms of other currencies, such a range *can* be found.

Bearing in mind this description, I am now prepared to make thirteen categorical statements (and a number of parenthetical remarks) about the system we now have.

1. We have developed the machinery for the administration of a new form of internationally managed gold standard which is capable of being used, and has been used, to implement a policy of relatively stable exchange rates between England, France, the United States and certain other countries that have not yet turned to exchange control, and yet which does not involve irrevocable commitment to a given system of rates.
2. The working of this machinery is dependent upon the maintenance of a fixed buying and a fixed selling price for gold in terms of one of the currencies governed by the system. (When we were off the gold standard in 1933 the French provided this essential element, but no system was built around the franc.)
3. Unless the exchanges in this system are dominated by long and persistent strength or weakness of one of its members, the machinery provides for stabilization within a certain range.

4. Since the focal point of the system is at present the United States and since the United States authorities impose a handling charge of 1/4 on gold purchases and sales, the limits of this range are established by a fluctuation in the sterling-dollar exchange of about seven or eight cents or a fluctuation of the London price of gold of about one shilling tenpence or some combination of the two.
5. The coöperation of all the countries in the system is necessary if the machinery is to work successfully, and this coöperation takes the form of willingness of the authorities to support their own currencies when they tend to move outside the general stabilization range by the sale of gold, and to support other currencies under the same circumstances by purchase of gold or of foreign exchange.
6. Long positions in foreign exchange taken as a result of these coöperative measures are not kept open if this can be avoided. As a matter of routine they are reversed within twenty-four hours by conversion into gold. Gold therefore offers to the authorities in each of the countries involved an insurance against the risk of holding any particular currency in the system, though not against the risk involved in a rapid appreciation of its own currency in terms of *all the others*. (The last point does not apply to the country which maintains a fixed price for gold. Gold also provides the authorities in each country with an option to buy most cheaply that one of the other currencies for which it has most need.
7. Under such a system the United States is *not* in the position in which it was from 1919 to 1924, despite appearances to the contrary. In those years there were no other bids in the London market competitive with the New York shipping parity, except those of India and the arts, and there were no offers except that of newly mined South African gold. Under the present system there are other bids and offers in the market for gold, and rel-

atively small movements in at least five exchanges make these bids and offers effective and the resulting gold distribution helps to hold a *system of rates* together as long as the countries who are working the machinery are in fact pursuing a policy of relative stability.

8. As long, however, as at the level chosen for the attempt at relative stabilization there is persistent pressure for the dollar to appreciate, these bids do not become effective and the appearance of a repetition of the situation of 1919 to 1924 is maintained.
9. The presence of such pressure so long continued may indicate that the level chosen for stabilization is untenable, and the present flexibility, to which the United States contributes by maintaining the fixed point around which the system is built and to which it can be adjusted, permits an orderly and sensible means of finding some level which can be defended.
10. That this is practical is indicated by the readjustment in sterling after September and the maintenance of the sterling rate fairly stable during the present even more severe crisis. (Parenthetically I do not think the transfer of gold to the Equalization Fund would have been followed by the weekly revaluation of the Bank of England Issue Department gold at market if continuous and violent fluctuations in the market price of gold had been expected.)
11. As long as stabilization of a system of exchange rates outside the world of wholly controlled currencies is part of practical policy, gold has peculiar technical advantages and will not be abandoned.
12. This conclusion is not invalidated by the example of the sterling countries whose exchanges are managed through London balances, for the world will not adopt a universal sterling exchange standard, nor in my opinion, will it adopt a universal dollar exchange standard.

13. The future of gold is bound up in the future of exchange stabilization in some form other than a world-wide dollar exchange standard, a world-wide system of exchange control or some division of the field between these two. (I should here like also to add parenthetically that I personally have not been convinced by arguments showing the superiority of flexible exchanges to fixed exchanges—chiefly because our first effort when we get free exchanges is to try to escape from their effects by some form of control, and because I think the universalization of exchange control offers incredible difficulties. Exchange control needs free exchanges to fill in the chinks as Mr. Hull has indignantly said. Also, after looking at the different kinds of marks, one cannot identify exchange control with exchange stability.)

These thirteen categorical statements boil down to one. My answer to the question as to whether there is anything in the *mechanism* of world gold distribution as we now have it which puts America in the position of an unwilling taker of all the world's gold is "No."

Yet we are getting incredible amounts of gold. Therefore this answer does not mean much if there are forces which make it likely that the continued use of this mechanism under present and reasonably foreseeable circumstances will bring us the rest of the world's gold. On this terrain I have to join rather serious issue with writers on the gold problem such as Professors Graham and Whittlesey, of Princeton, who in an article in the April, 1939, issue of *Foreign Affairs* seem to me to take a very remarkable view of the causes of the gold movement to the United States. They say

First: "The argument that the devaluation of the American dollar has been an important factor in diverting gold to the United States is quite without foundation."

Second: "Since gold is being sent here *not to extinguish American claims on the outside world* but to establish foreign claims against this country, we are, without any intent on our part to assume the role, being forced into a debtor position on international account."

Third: "Rates of exchange have no longer any decisive influence upon gold movements, even though gold movements still have a marked influence upon rates of exchange."

Each of these statements is given a supporting argument, and I hope I am not acting unfairly in not giving these arguments and meeting them in detail, but there is not time and after all I simply wish to give my view on the positive content of these statements, for that bears directly on the probable future of gold.

It seems to me really fantastic to say that the devaluation of the American dollar did not contribute to bringing gold here. By that devaluation we forced upon the world an untenable and artificial system of exchange rates. *While* we were doing so we were directly responsible for a great movement of gold to this country. I should like to read from the Annual Bullion Letter of Messrs. Samuel Montagu and Co. for 1934.

The drastic alteration in the United States Treasury gold price, made as it was for reasons of internal economics rather than because of any weakness in the world value of the dollar, created opportunities for gold arbitrage with the United States of America on a scale, and with a margin of profit, hitherto beyond the wildest dreams of the arbitrageur.

Immediately following the announcement, substantial shipments were arranged by the next available steamers leaving Europe for New York. For a few days, however, many operators held back, there being considerable speculation as to the exact nature of the new conditions attaching to the purchase of gold. When it was realized without doubt that the United States were again back on an effective gold standard and willing to take all gold tendered from abroad at the new statutory rate, a flow of gold commenced to that country which quickly assumed flood proportions, only abating towards the end of February.

Never before has such a huge movement of gold taken place in so short a time. Accommodation on all mail steamers was booked well ahead and many other vessels other than the regular liners were pressed into service as bullion carriers. The demand for insurance caused premiums to rise sharply and as much as 20s. per cent. was paid on occasion, compared with the normal market rate 1s. per cent. Indeed it was the difficulty of placing insurance beyond certain amounts on any one steamer that limited the consignments carried, rather than shortage of space in vessels. The United States Treasury officials were overwhelmed by the inrush and at first there was considerable delay in making settlement for gold tendered.[1]

At the new valuation of $35 per ounce these imports amounted in February alone to $454 millions, of which $239 millions came from London and $124 millions from France. The gold losses of the Bank of France during the month were over 3 milliards, and American demand carried all before it in the London market. Under this tremendous support sterling and francs rose substantially in dollars, but the adjustment of the dollar-franc rate to the new parity was delayed by the underlying weakness of the franc. *After* the new system was established doubts as to whether it could be maintained *caused* further large imports of gold to America. The Federal Reserve Bulletin estimates that the foreign funds that came into this country from France, Switzerland, the Netherlands, and England as a result of gold-bloc crises, up to September, 1936, and as a result of the gold scare in 1937 aggregated by the middle of 1937 over one billion dollars. We were certainly not innocent bystanders in this. We caused the gold bloc crises and we caused the gold scare in the sense that neither would have taken place without dollar devaluation. In my opinion, moreover, the full readjustment of the exchanges to the situation created by dollar devaluation has only just been worked out by the last devaluation of the franc and the recent 8 percent decline in the pound sterling.

In the second place it is definitely wrong to infer or imply that the bulk of the gold which we received in recent years was sent to us to force us to become unwilling borrowers. Leaving aside the fact that the capital movement comes first, influences the exchanges, and that, *as a result of an effort to stabilize these exchanges,* gold

[1] Messrs. Samuel Montagu & Co., *Annual Bullion Letter* (1934), p. 3.

comes in, it is well known that a third or more of the capital movement represents American initiative in the form of the reduction of American balances abroad and the sale of American-owned foreign securities. Gold so attracted *does* represent gold sent here to extinguish American claims on the outside world. So also does the gold that came to us in 1938 as the result of our sudden development of a merchandise export surplus of about a billion dollars, leaving us with a substantial net debit on current visible and invisible trade including interest. From 1934 to 1937 there had been no substantial pressure on the exchanges from these major items in our balance of payments, but when this large debit developed in 1938, gold surely came to extinguish American claims abroad.

It is of course true that we have had to take a lot of gold to permit foreigners to establish dollar claims here. The Federal Reserve Bulletin says we have a billion and a half of refugee capital from abroad, but that explains only a fairly small part of our import since 1934 of seven and a half billions in gold. It is not true that we have been gorged with gold because we are being forced into debt to foreigners. We have a direct responsibility for the bulk of the gold inflow, though not for all of it.

As I have indicated, part of this gold came to us as the result of the extraordinary drop in our merchandise imports in 1938. It would, I think, be absurd to attribute this to a failure of the automatic price adjustments attributed to the pre-war gold standard. The decline in imports which brought us this part of our gold stock was surely due to our own inability to solve our own fiscal and economic problems.

For five years we have imported gold to the tune of a billion and a half a year. Whether the causes which have brought this gold here will operate as strongly in the future as in the recent past depends partly on whether the peculiar situation which accompanied and followed the devaluation of the dollar in 1934 will be repeated; this I consider very unlikely. Most economists would, I am sure, agree that further dollar devaluation would be folly, but even if we committed that folly, foreign reactions to it would be different. A continued gold inflow on the same grand scale depends further on whether we are going periodically to develop sudden export surpluses of the order of a billion dollars as in 1938; whether fresh repatriations of our own foreign investments and receipt of refugee capital will continue on the present scale, or an even larger scale, to make up for the change in the interest item in our balance of payments which they entail; and finally whether it is or will be true that rates of exchange no longer have any decisive influence upon gold movements.

This brings me back to where I started—the description of our present managed international gold bullion standard. If all attempts to maintain a system of relatively stable exchanges with the aid of gold shipments are abandoned, and we continue to buy all gold offered at a fixed price, and the other monetary authorities are willing to give up permanently the present conveniences which the possession of gold gives them, and if all the other ifs which I have just suggested concerning the causes of gold movements to America come true, why then of course the pessimistic view of the future of gold is justified. But I think this is a very long series of improbabilities, though I do not say impossibilities.

Whatever we may think of the future, we *have* received a vast quantity of gold which we do not want. We have given something for it. Have we been completely swindled in this exchange? I think not completely swindled.

To the extent that gold has come to us as a result of dollar devaluation we have *created for ourselves* part of our very difficult problem of potential domestic inflation.

Though we have given a large amount of goods for gold which we do not need, our main payment has been in the form of evidences of debt or the cancellation of debts due us. As far as the debts we have incurred in exchange for gold are concerned we *may* pay some of them back with the gold we have, but probably not much. We are more likely to pay them back in goods. Goods for gold on this scale is not an advantageous exchange.

Far more important, in my opinion, is the fact that we have taken gold in preference to sacrificing other values by violent adjustments in our trade through thoroughly disrupted exchanges. We have become a central cog in a machine which has maintained in a period of unexampled crisis some semblance of an orderly system of exchange rates. We have been willing to allow orderly readjustments in that system so that now it seems in a position where we can hope to maintain it approximately as it is for some considerable time. We have made it possible, moreover, for very large movements of frightened capital to take place without disrupting the exchanges to the point where, for example, our reciprocal trade program would have to be abandoned.

These are substantial offsets to the inconveniences caused us by gold imports, particularly since we are not helpless to deal with the consequences of our gold holdings. I do not need to come to a Columbia banking seminar to indicate the vast credit control powers with which we are equipped, or to suggest that there have been other inflationary measures which create potential danger and for which we are ourselves wholly responsible.

We must, I think, accept the already realized consequences of the follies of the past whereby we and other countries have misused gold in almost incredible degree; draw a line around the great mass of gold which we now have; and set out from now on without thought of gold redistribution to coöperate in the management of the system of international exchange regulation which we now have and to improve on it. The most important element in such coöperation is not the technical one I have been talking about, but is setting our own house in order and maintaining stable credit conditions in our own country. There are alternatives of course, completely free exchanges, or exchange control, but I do not think we will embrace them.

I think that the probable future of gold is that we shall accept, without trying to evade, the consequences of our past mistakes, and build a humbler and more constructive role for gold in our international dealings in the future—provided we have peace. If we have war we cannot say that anything that we are now familiar with has a future that we can predict.

W. D. Whittemore

The Work of the Export-Import Bank

THE EXPORT-IMPORT Bank of Washington is an agency of the United States Government established by the President, under Executive Order Number 6,581, pursuant to authority granted to him by Section 2 of Title 1 of the National Industrial Recovery Act "to aid in financing and to facilitate exports and imports and the exchange of commodities between the United States, its territories or insular possessions and any foreign country or agencies or nationals thereof." Those words practically preclude the bank's doing any strictly domestic banking. We are concerned only with the import and export of commodities. The bank was first established in 1934, to finance expected trade in large volume with the Soviet Union. The United States at that time recognized the Soviet government, and it was expected that there would be a considerable volume of exports going to that country. It was expected also that the Soviet Union would take some action toward repaying the pre-war and previous debts. That was never done. The bank did no business for eighteen months.

The Second Export-Import Bank was formed in March, 1934, to aid Cuban trade and commerce. It was decided that it might branch out into financing exports. That bank did a certain amount of business, but it was liquidated in 1936. Then there became only one Export-Import Bank, which is the one existing today, its name being the "Export-Import Bank of Washington."

The present Export-Import Bank has had its life extended twice, first to June 16, 1937; it was then to expire on June 30, 1939. In

March, 1939, its life was again extended, this time to June 30, 1941. Previous to the latter extension, there was no legal limit placed on the bank's lending power. But in the discussion this year there was considerable reference made to the possibility of making political loans, involving the country in foreign complications. Therefore the Congress thought it expedient to place a limitation, which now stands at $100,000,000; we may not have more than $100,000,000 outstanding in obligations to the bank.

The bank is incorporated under a District of Columbia charter. The actual powers are very broad, but must be read in connection with the few words I quoted in the beginning. In connection with the purpose for which it was created, the bank is authorized to do a general banking business: to purchase, sell, negotiate, with or without its endorsement, notes, drafts, bills of exchange, acceptances, including bankers' acceptances, cables, transfers by cable, and other evidences of indebtedness, and, with the approval of the Secretary of the Treasury, to borrow money and to rediscount notes, drafts, bills of exchange, and other evidences of debt; to purchase and sell securities, including obligations of the United States or any state thereof, but not including the purchase with its funds of any stock in any other corporation; to issue letters of credit, to purchase and sell coin, bullion, and exchange; to lend money, and to do and to perform the necessary functions permitted by law in conducting such enterprise or business. Obviously, that is very broad. But these things can be done only in connection with the imports and exports of the country.

The control of the bank rests in a Board of Trustees of eleven members. The Board of Trustees consists of two representatives of the State Department, two from the Department of Commerce, one from the Treasury Department, the President of the Bank, one from the Department of Agriculture, and four from the Reconstruction Finance Corporation. The present board consists of:

Harry L. Hopkins, Secretary of Commerce

R. Walton Moore, Counselor, Department of State

Wayne C. Taylor, Assistant Secretary of the Treasury

Warren Lee Pierson, President, Export-Import Bank

W. J. Johnson, Assistant Chief, Examining Division, Reconstruction Finance Corporation

H. L. Mulligan, Treasurer, Reconstruction Finance Corporation

Herbert Feis, Adviser on International Economic Affairs, Department of State

Russell L. Snodgrass, Assistant General Counsel, Reconstruction Finance Corporation

Albert G. Black, Chief, Bureau of Agricultural Economics, Department of Agriculture

Jesse H. Jones, Chairman, Reconstruction Finance Corporation

Richard C. Patterson, Jr., Assistant Secretary of Commerce.

The capital of the bank consists of $1,000,000 common stock and, at the present time, $45,000,000 preferred stock. The common stock is held jointly by the Secretary of Commerce and the Secretary of State for the benefit of the United States. The preferred stock is all held by the Reconstruction Finance Corporation. Any further capital that may be required by the bank, up to the $100,000,000, is to be provided by the Reconstruction Finance Corporation.

It may be of interest if I speak of the amount of business that the bank has handled. Since its creation, the Export-Import Bank, including the Second Bank dissolved in 1936, made $229,500,000 commitments, of which $99,000,000 were canceled. This, I think, was because applicants found they did not require them or found the necessary credit from private sources. In other cases, I have reason to believe that after we have agreed to finance a certain piece of business, the manufacturer either handles it himself or his commercial bank reasons that if the credit is satisfactory to the Export-Import Bank, it is good enough for it. The bank has disbursed nearly $68,000,000, of which $40,000,000 has been repaid, leaving the sum of $28,000,000 outstanding at the present time, all of which is current. In addition to that, we have considerable commitments to make further disbursements as and when required during the near future.

The policy of the bank is to compete in no way with the commercial banks of the country for the business which they can or should handle. In pursuance of this policy, we deliberately keep our charges high. We do not wish to take any business that any of the private commercial banks would take. We come into the picture only when the transaction is one which they do not wish to undertake or which they feel they could not undertake, but which at the same time we consider more than reasonably safe and both beneficial to this country and to the economy of the foreign country. So far, our record has been fortunate.

Following that policy, we find ourselves obliged to do certain things that are not quite in accordance with the tenets of commercial banking. Our exporters abroad have to meet the competition of foreign nations which indulge in subsidies and which engage in writing export credit insurance. Our exporters have to meet that competition, and, in a way, we have endeavored to help them. We cannot write insurance. It is a question as to whether we could issue a guarantee. We try to avoid that word by financing a portion of certain shipments, on a basis without recourse to the exporter or to the manufacturer. We do not go to a full 100 percent. Fifty percent is customary, 60 percent is occasional, perhaps 65, and with one exception 75 percent is the maximum. We feel that the exporter himself must have a substantial stake in the business and that under no circumstance should we be called upon to finance or to insure the manufacturer's profit. And when we say "profit," we disregard all but his actual, direct costs. We do not permit him to insure his overhead costs. We try to keep our participation down to and even below 65 or 75 percent. We also try to get other banks to participate with us, even if it is without recourse. The formula is: 40 percent with other banks, 40 percent with us, and Mr. Manufacturer ought to take 20 percent. We find it hard to get the other banks to take 40 percent. They want to handle the business, but want us to take the risk.

Some people wonder what we do, in the Export-Import Bank. Sometimes we wonder ourselves. But it can be summed up in one word—"work." We have a small staff of thirteen, including the office boy. I might say that the activities of the bank are confined largely to two major fields: the financing on short-term accommodations of the export of agricultural commodities, and long-term financing of the export of industrial products. In the short-term type of financing, of six months or perhaps nine months, we have had an increasing number of demands. Our activities have been mostly confined to cotton.

The commercial banks hold, and rightly, that extension of credit for a longer period than three months, or perhaps four at the outside, in connection with the export of a consumption commodity like cotton, is tantamount to extending a working-capital loan to the foreign spinners or dealers, for the period in excess of the three or four months. Our justification for allowing six months or nine months is this: we have an enormous stock of cotton which we want to move; therefore we feel that with respect to those countries in which the exchange condition is acute, we can properly extend credit for the longer term, in order to allow time to spin the cotton, weave it, export the manufactured goods, and thus derive the exchange with which to repay our advance. Those countries which have a free exchange have not sought the longer-term facilities. Our experience has been very satisfactory; in no case has any of the countries taken advantage of the option of a three months' extension.

We have been bombarded lately with requests to finance wheat in the same way. The buyers want credit for anywhere from six months to two and one-half years. We say "No, wheat is strictly a local consumption commodity and is not to be processed into exportable manufactured goods." At the same time, this wheat which they want is subsidy wheat, and our feeling is that since they are getting the wheat so cheaply, there is no reason why we should sell it on long-term credit. Let them pay cash for it.

There are a number of things that are banned on our list. We do not attempt to finance any of those articles which, from the point of view of the joint resolution of May 1, 1937, known as the Neutrality Act, could be considered as being war materials, munitions, or implements of war. Aeroplanes are accordingly banned.

By way of following our policy of assisting merchants with limited capital, the bank established a line of credit to the amount of $100,000, and later increased it to $200,000. Under this, the bank can make allotments, not exceeding $10,000, to a firm or to an individual, to finance exports. Borrowers must have first-class references, business ability, experience, and must themselves have a certain amount of capital.

Here are a few typical transactions: Fountain pens to South America, a matter of $3,000; for the Republic of Cuba, coinage operations, under which we purchased the silver here, arranged with the Treasury Department that it should be coined at the Mint and shipped to Cuba; pipe and water meters to Mexico; printing presses; rails; cotton to Italy; water-purifying equipment; ice-making machinery; tobacco; cotton and wheat to China; can-making machinery to Brazil; farm machinery to Chile; meats, game, pheasants, partridge, from Central Europe and the Far East. We have had transactions involving shipments to and from thirty-two different countries, and, within the last year alone, nineteen different countries. The bank has assisted in financing sales of tobacco to Spain; cotton to Czechoslovakia, Germany, Latvia, Poland, and China; and rail equipment and machinery to Colombia, Costa Rica,

Brazil, British India, China, and Mexico. These are our major export transactions.

In addition to these, we have had a few special transactions. Last year we set up a commitment to finance a program of public works for Haiti. The provision was that all the machinery was to be shipped from the United States. The bank agreed with an American engineering firm to discount notes to be issued to it by the Haitian government, in payment for planning and carrying out a program of public works within the Republic of Haiti. These public works, which were designed to be—and which I think undoubtedly will be—decidedly beneficial to the economy of the Republic of Haiti, included roads, irrigation works, and the improvement of harbor facilities.

Two or three years ago, Brazil found itself in a decidedly frozen position. The bank helped to unfreeze it. Notes, to be paid over a period of five years to refund the arrears, were issued. We finally said that we would take such notes as were offered to us. The idea was that by purchasing these notes we repaired the working capital of the holders of the notes. Payments have been made promptly.

More recently we undertook another large project—a commitment of $19,200,000 was set up in favor of the Banco do Brasil. This actually was another unfreezing arrangement, but instead of the government of Brazil issuing its own notes, payable over a period of time, we are making credits available, against which the Banco do Brasil will draw. This line is a little different from some of the others. It is a commitment to create dollar exchange. It was arranged that the operation should be handled by a number of American banks, designated by the Banco do Brasil, which will draw drafts at ninety days or three months' sight. The American banks will accept these drafts, discount them, and credit the proceeds to the Banco do Brasil. The Banco do Brasil is at liberty to draw against that balance. At the end of ninety days it must pay 10 percent of its indebtedness in cash and may renew the balance. At the end of the next ninety-day period, it must again pay 10 percent in cash and may again renew the balance, repeating the process each ninety days until the advance is entirely repaid.

Somewhat earlier I mentioned that we were financing cotton to Italy and Poland. Those credits rest on the responsibility of banks in those countries. Here again we arrange with banks in this country to handle operations for us. An Italian bank or a Polish bank writes or cables to one of our agent banks, instructing it to open a letter of credit in favor of the shipper who has sold cotton. This letter of credit will stipulate that drafts are to be drawn at six months' sight, and will designate the documents which are to accompany the drafts. In many cases the cotton is already in Europe or afloat, and perhaps the documents are in the hands of some other financial institution. The American bank accepts the shipper's drafts, pays him the face amount, charging the discount to the European institution. The foreign bank has the option of a three months' extension, if it wishes to take advantage of it.

We are also financing shipments of tires to Iran, but in this case the technique is slightly different. The Iranian bank had previously opened a letter of credit in favor of the American shipper, but the shipper did not care to carry even that risk and wanted us to negotiate his drafts "without recourse." We agreed to do this, to the extent of 65 percent. In this case the shipper draws his drafts, hands them to the bank through which the credit was advised, which bank then forwards drafts and documents to the Iranian bank. The Iranian bank in due course cables advice of acceptance of the drafts, and at that point the New York bank, for our account, advances 65 percent of the face amount, after deduction of discount and charges. We could not take such drafts "without recourse" prior to acceptance, as in such case we would be purchasing a piece of paper without any name thereon to which we could look for protection.

Sometimes we have some wild proposals offered to us. A gentleman came into the office some four or five weeks ago. He had conceived the idea that a large number of men and mechanics could be transported to a foreign country in eastern Europe. In that country, he and his associates would obtain a grant of land amounting to about $25,000,000 in value, which was to be in the nature of a payment or an offset against that country's indebtedness to the United States Government. This land was to include water-power facilities, some forestry area, and some agricultural land. Having this land, he needed some working capital. He wanted to build a series of warehouses in various ports, which would act as distributing centers for the merchandise which they were going to export and import. And then he needed working capital to pay wages. Of the salaries and wages, he proposed to pay 80 percent in cash and 20 percent in the stock of the corporation, both for officers and laborers. A number of positions were to pay $10,000, $8,000, $7,000 per year, and he finally did get down as low as $1,500. But when I asked the direct question of how much of the capital he and his associates were prepared to furnish, I found that they were not furnishing any.

Another gentleman came in and told us that there was any amount of high-grade iron ore in Brazil, waiting to be exploited (which we knew already). He claimed to have a concession or a title, and he wished to develop the mine and at the same time to build a short connecting railroad and to double-track an existing railroad. The project would involve the expenditure of some $50,000,000. I am certain that the ore was there, but this gentleman wished us to put up the entire capital with which to develop it.

Some operations which do not involve a great deal of clerical work we handle ourselves. We have only a small staff, and we do not maintain so-called operating departments as do commercial banks. We have not the staff nor the organization to handle transactions which involve considerable clerical work in the way of examination of documents, bookkeeping, and so forth. Therefore we arrange with commercial banks, usually the bank of the importer or exporter, to conduct operations for us, as agents. The interest, discount, or other income arising from such operations is divided between the agent bank and ourselves on a prearranged basis which is mutually satisfactory.

Index

Bei Fragen zur Produktsicherheit wenden Sie sich bitte an:
If you have any questions regarding product safety,
please contact:

Walter de Gruyter GmbH
Genthiner Straße 13
10785 Berlin
productsafety@degruyterbrill.com